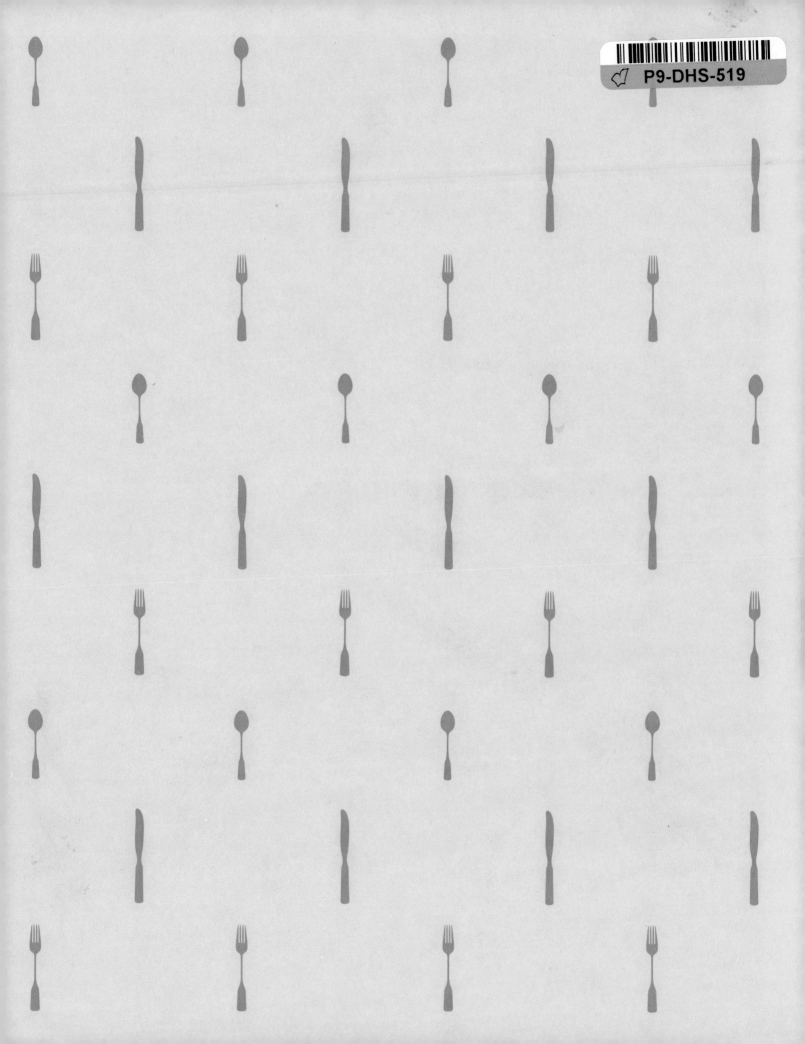

Fresh Ways
with Pasta

Time-Life Books Inc.
is a wholly owned subsidiary of
TIME INCORPORATED

FOUNDER: Henry R. Luce 1898-1967

Editor-in-Chief: Henry Anatole Grunwald
President: J. Richard Munro
Chairman of the Board: Ralph P. Davidson
Corporate Editor: Ray Cave
Group Vice President, Books: Reginald K. Brack Jr.
Vice President, Books: George Artandi

COVER
Lobster and collard greens nestle among ripple-edged mafalda, a slender relative of lasagne. Both the greens and the pasta were cooked in water flavored by the lobster shells and juices; the lobster meat, greens and pasta were then tossed with a little brown butter and lemon or lime juice just before serving (recipe, page 79).

TIME-LIFE BOOKS INC.

EDITOR: George Constable
Executive Editor: George Daniels
Editorial General Manager: Neal Goff
Director of Design: Louis Klein
Director of Editorial Resources: Phyllis K. Wise
Editorial Board: Dale M. Brown, Roberta Conlan,
Ellen Phillips, Donia Ann Steele, Rosalind Stubenberg,
Kit van Tulleken, Henry Woodhead
Director of Research and Photography:
John Conrad Weiser

PRESIDENT: Reginald K. Brack Jr.
Executive Vice Presidents: John M. Fahey Jr.,
Christopher T. Linen
Senior Vice President: James L. Mercer
Vice Presidents: Stephen L. Bair, Edward Brash,
Ralph J. Cuomo, Juanita T. James, Wilhelm R. Saake,
Robert H. Smith, Paul R. Stewart, Leopoldo Toralballa

Editorial Operations
Copy Chief: Diane Ullius
Editorial Operations: Caroline A. Boubin (manager)
Production: Celia Beattie
Quality Control: James J. Cox (director)
Library: Louise D. Forstall

Correspondents: Elisabeth Kraemer-Singh (Bonn);
Dorothy Bacon (London); Maria Vincenza Aloisi,
Josephine du Brusle (Paris); Ann Natanson (Rome).

Library of Congress Cataloguing in Publication Data
Main entry under title:
Fresh ways with pasta.
    (Healthy home cooking)
    Includes index.
    1. Cookery (Macaroni) I. Time-Life Books. II. Series.
TX809.M17F74 1986   641.8'22   85-31826
ISBN 0-8094-5812-8
ISBN 0-8094-5813-6 (lib. bdg.)

For information on and a full description of any Time-Life Books
series, please write:
Reader Information
Time-Life Books
541 North Fairbanks Court
Chicago, Illinois 60611

HEALTHY HOME COOKING

SERIES DIRECTOR: Dale M. Brown
Deputy Editor: Barbara Fleming
Series Administrator: Elise Ritter Gibson
Designer: Herbert H. Quarmby
Picture Editor: Sally Collins
Photographer: Renée Comet
Text Editor: Allan Fallow
Editorial Assistant: Rebecca C. Christoffersen

Editorial Staff for *Fresh Ways with Pasta:*
Book Manager: Barbara Sause
Assistant Picture Editor: Scarlet Cheng
Writer: Margery A. duMond
Researcher-Writer: Jean Getlein
Copy Coordinators: Marfé Ferguson, Elizabeth Graham
Picture Coordinator: Linda Yates
Photographer's Assistant: Rina M. Ganassa

Special Contributors: Mary Jane Blandford (food
purchasing), Carol Gvozdich (nutrient analysis), Nancy
Lendved (props), Ann Ready (text), CiCi Williamson
(microwave section)

THE COOKS

ADAM DE VITO began his cooking apprenticeship at L'Auberge Chez François near Washington, D.C., when he was only 14. He has worked at Washington's Le Pavillon restaurant, taught with cookbook author Madeleine Kamman, and conducted classes at L'Académie de Cuisine in Maryland.

HENRY GROSSI, who started his cooking career with a New York caterer, earned a Grand Diplôme at the École de Cuisine La Varenne in Paris. He then served as the school's assistant director and as its North American business and publications coordinator.

JOHN T. SHAFFER is a graduate of The Culinary Institute of America at Hyde Park, New York. He has had broad experience as a chef, including five years at The Four Seasons Hotel in Washington, D.C., where he was *chef saucier* at Aux Beaux Champs restaurant.

THE CONSULTANT

CAROL CUTLER lives in Washington, D.C., and is the prizewinning author of many cookbooks, including *The Six-Minute Soufflé and Other Culinary Delights* and *Pâté: The New Main Course for the 80's.* During the 12 years she lived in France, she studied at the Cordon Bleu and the École des Trois Gourmandes, as well as with private chefs. She is a member of the Cercle des Gourmettes as well as a charter member and past president of Les Dames d'Escoffier.

THE NUTRITION CONSULTANT

JANET TENNEY has been involved in nutrition and consumer affairs since she received her master's degree in human nutrition from Columbia University. She is the manager for developing and implementing nutritional programs for a major chain of supermarkets in the Washington, D.C., area.

SPECIAL CONSULTANT

Sharon Farrington, a food writer and consultant specializing in Asian cuisines, developed most of the recipes for the Asian-pasta section of this book. Raised in Oregon, she learned how to prepare Asian food while living in Thailand in the mid-1970s. During that time, she traveled through Laos, Cambodia, Vietnam, Burma, Malaysia and Indonesia. She is a regular contributor to the food section of *The Washington Post* and teaches at L'Académie de Cuisine in Maryland.

Other Publications:

UNDERSTANDING COMPUTERS
YOUR HOME
THE ENCHANTED WORLD
THE KODAK LIBRARY OF CREATIVE PHOTOGRAPHY
GREAT MEALS IN MINUTES
THE CIVIL WAR
PLANET EARTH
COLLECTOR'S LIBRARY OF THE CIVIL WAR
THE EPIC OF FLIGHT
THE GOOD COOK
WORLD WAR II
HOME REPAIR AND IMPROVEMENT
THE OLD WEST

This volume is one of a series of illustrated cookbooks
that emphasize the preparation of healthful dishes for
today's weight-conscious, nutrition-minded eaters.

Fresh Ways with Pasta

BY

THE EDITORS OF TIME-LIFE BOOKS

TIME-LIFE BOOKS / ALEXANDRIA, VIRGINIA

Contents

Tomato Fettuccine with Artichokes and Mint

Crab Pillows

Pasta Shells and Scallops

Egg Noodles with Poppy Seeds, Yogurt and Mushrooms

3 The World of Asian Noodles 100

Japanese Summer Noodles with Shrimp

*Spaghetti with Fresh Basil,
Pine Nuts and Cheese*

Duckling Dumplings and Ginger-Plum Sauce

4 Pasta in the Microwave Oven 130

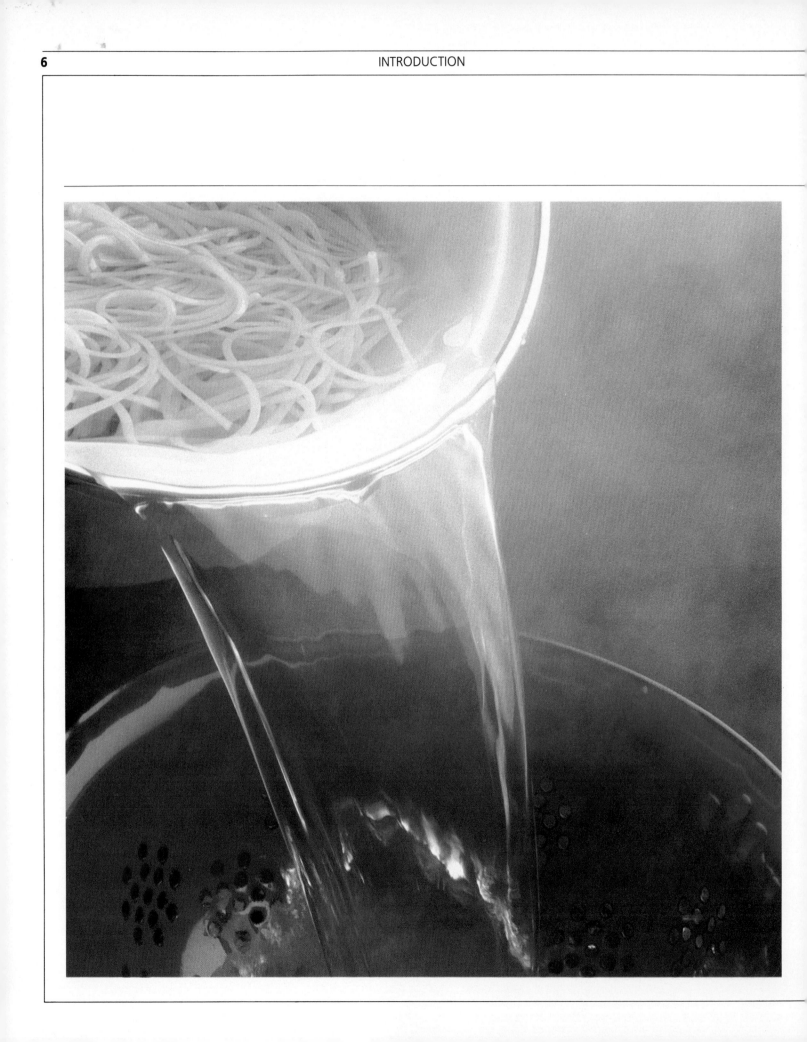

Bravo, Pasta!

Pasta is easy, and pasta is cheap. Better yet, it is good for you. It has become the preferred food of athletes before a meet or game, packing its own wallop of energy. And weight-conscious cooks can delight in the knowledge that pasta is not the fattening food everyone once thought it was. Americans now eat about 11 pounds of pasta per capita a year, almost double the quantity consumed a decade or so ago, and the volume keeps rising.

What makes pasta exceptional? Its wheat-flour starch, for one thing. A complex carbohydrate, the starch provides as much energy as pure protein. Moreover, pasta is easy to digest, and it provides a long-lasting feeling of satisfaction that can be a boon to girth-watchers by curtailing their appetites. The wonder is that a food so sustaining should have relatively few calories: A cup of cooked spaghetti (about five ounces) contains a slender 210 calories, less than half those in a five-ounce portion of sirloin steak.

Pasta has further advantages. Its protein is made up of six of the eight essential amino acids; for pasta to be a complete food, all it needs is a little meat sauce or grated cheese to round out and enhance its protein. Pasta also contains niacin, thiamin and riboflavin, calcium and iron, and fiber. Sauced wisely and well, a pasta dish served with a fresh green salad, and followed by a fruit dessert, is a perfect meal, high in satisfaction and nutrition.

Pasta's Infinite Variety

Pasta is traditionally defined as a wheat-paste food made from flour and water. This book stretches that definition to include Asian noodles, which can be made from rice, mung beans, buckwheat or other ingredients, as well as wheat. The dried commercial variety is generally produced from protein-rich semolina, the coarsely ground endosperm of kernels of hard durum wheat. When water is added to semolina flour and the dough is worked, gluten is developed and a resilient dough is formed. This dough is then extruded or stamped out under great pressure by machine, and the resulting pasta is carefully dried. Occasionally eggs are added to yield the egg noodles so popular in Central European dishes. Most dried pasta has a long shelf life and can be safely stored in a dry place for up to two years without losing flavor.

While dried pasta is best when made with semolina, fresh pasta can be prepared at home with regular flour. In this book the fresh pasta recipes call for unbleached all-purpose flour, or finely milled semolina flour combined with the all-purpose flour. Fortunately, finely milled semolina flour is becoming increasingly available in markets (the coarsely milled type absorbs water poorly and is difficult to work with by hand). The recipes tell how much water to add to the dough — but since flours differ in their ability to absorb moisture, more may be used if the dough proves too stiff to roll out easily by hand or through a pasta machine.

The four sections that follow sing the praises of pasta. Though they concentrate on pasta as a main course, they also present recipes for pasta appetizers and side dishes. The first section deals with fresh pasta and shows, in a series of step-by-step photographs, how to make and shape pasta and how to stuff several kinds with savory fillings. The second section concentrates on dried pasta, including egg noodles and North African couscous. The third delves into Asian noodles and dumplings, and it too utilizes photographs to demonstrate methods of making and shaping them. The fourth section puts the microwave oven to work cooking a variety of pasta dishes; for a couple of these, sauce ingredients and uncooked pasta go into the oven together and emerge minutes later ready to eat. Since pasta comes in a dizzying range of sizes and shapes, pages 44-45 and 102-103 illustrate all the types called for in the recipes and identify them by the names under which you are likely to find them in markets.

In buying dried pasta, examine the label to be certain that the pasta has been produced with semolina. Pastas made with all or part farina, the coarsely ground endosperm of any wheat except durum, should be avoided because they turn pasty during the boiling. When cooked, good pasta can swell to nearly three times its size and possesses a slightly nutty, sweet flavor.

As for cooking, two rules apply: Use a lot of boiling water and be sure not to overcook the pasta. (For more detailed instructions, see the box at right.) While almost all the recipes in this book call for salting the water, the quantity used is less than that required by many other cookbooks. And cooks should bear in mind that the salt is highly diluted when adequate water is used and that a relatively small amount of salt is absorbed by the pasta. Leave it out entirely, and the pasta will be insipid, unless coupled with an intensely flavored sauce. Some cooks find that a little lemon juice in the water makes a fairly good substitute for salt.

The Question of Portion Size

For consistency's sake, this book employs the same standard measure for a single serving as most pasta manufacturers recommend — two ounces dried for five ounces cooked. Most people will probably agree that with a food as popular as pasta five ounces constitute rather scant eating when presented as a main course. Cooks should feel free to prepare and serve as much pasta as they want so long as they take into account the greater calories the larger portion entails and the caloric value of the rest of the meal, as well as that of the remainder of the day's eating.

The recipes for accompanying sauces list fresh ingredients for maximum flavor and nutrition, but because juicy, well-ripened tomatoes frequently are unavailable, the recipes offer the option of using whole canned tomatoes. The whole are preferred to

The Key to Better Eating

This book, like others in the Healthy Home Cooking series, presents an analysis of nutrients contained in a single serving of each dish, listed beside the recipe itself, as at right. Actual counts for calories, protein, cholesterol, total fat, saturated fat (the kind that increases the body's blood cholesterol) and sodium are given.

Healthy Home Cooking addresses the concerns of today's weight-conscious, health-minded cooks by providing recipes that fall within guidelines set by nutritionists. The secret to eating well, of course, has to do with maintaining a balance of foods in the diet; most Americans consume too much sugar and salt, too much fat and too many calories, even too much protein.

Interpreting the Chart

The chart below shows the National Research Council's recommended dietary allowances of calories and protein for healthy men, women and children, along with the council's recommendations for the "safe and adequate" maximum intake of sodium. Although the council has not established recommendations for cholesterol or fat, the chart does include what the National Institutes of Health and the American Heart Association consider the daily maximum allowable amounts of these for healthy people.

The volumes in the Healthy Home Cooking series do not purport to be diet books, nor do they focus on health foods. Rather, they express a commonsense approach to cooking that uses salt, sugar, cream, butter and oil in moderation while employing other ingredients that also provide flavor and satisfaction. Herbs, spices, aromatic vegetables, fruits and peels, and juices, wines and vinegars are all used toward this end.

The recipes make few unusual demands. Naturally they call for fresh ingredients, offering substitutes when these are unavailable. (Only the original ingredient is calculated in the nutrient analysis, however.) Most of the pastas and the sauce ingredients can be

Calories **285**
Protein **11g.**
Cholesterol **4mg.**
Total fat **6g.**
Saturated fat **2g.**
Sodium **352mg.**

found in any well-stocked supermarket; the exceptions — particularly some of the Asian noodles and condiments — can be bought in specialty shops or ethnic stores.

In planning a meal, the cook using the recipes should consider what the rest of the meal is likely to contribute nutritionally. The cook should also bear in mind that moderate portions are always recommended.

In Healthy Home Cooking's test kitchens, heavy-bottomed pots and pans are used to guard against burning the food whenever a small amount of oil is used and where there is danger of the food adhering to the hot surface, but nonstick pans can be utilized as well. Both safflower oil and virgin olive oil are favored for sautéing. Safflower was chosen because it is the most highly polyunsaturated vegetable fat available in supermarkets, and polyunsaturated fats reduce blood cholesterol. Virgin olive oil is used because it has a fine fruity flavor lacking in the lesser grade known as "pure." In addition, it is — like all olive oil — high in monounsaturated fats, which do not increase blood cholesterol and, according to recent research, may even lower it. Sometimes the two oils are combined, with the olive oil contributing its fruitiness to the safflower oil. When virgin olive oil is unavailable, "pure" may be substituted.

About Cooking Times

To help the cook plan ahead, Healthy Home Cooking takes time into account in its recipes. While recognizing that everyone cooks at a different speed, and that stoves and ovens differ, the series provides approximate "working" and "total" times for every dish. Working time stands for the actual minutes spent on preparation; total time includes unattended cooking time, as well as time devoted to marinating, steeping or soaking ingredients. Since the recipes emphasize fresh foods, they may take a bit longer to prepare than "quick and easy" dishes that call for canned or packaged products, but the payoff in flavor and often in nutrition should compensate for the little extra time involved.

Recommended Dietary Guidelines

		Average Daily Intake		Maximum Daily Intake			
		CALORIES	PROTEIN *grams*	CHOLESTEROL *milligrams*	TOTAL FAT *grams*	SATURATED FAT *grams*	SODIUM *milligrams*
Children	7-10	2400	22	240	80	27	1800
Females	11-14	2200	37	220	73	24	2700
	15-18	2100	44	210	70	23	2700
	19-22	2100	44	300	70	23	3300
	23-50	2000	44	300	67	22	3300
	51-75	1800	44	300	60	20	3300
Males	11-14	2700	36	270	90	30	2700
	15-18	2800	56	280	93	31	2700
	19-22	2900	56	300	97	32	3300
	23-50	2700	56	300	90	30	3300
	51-75	2400	56	300	80	27	3300

canned puréed or sliced as having better flavor; after draining, they can be easily puréed or chopped. A well-made tomato sauce is one of dining's great pleasures, and it should not be degraded by being dusted with inferior pregrated Parmesan. Freshly grated, aromatic cheese is in order.

Now that pasta is no longer being maligned as a fattening food, it may be enjoyed to the full. But people should guard against raising the calorie count of a dish by going overboard on the sauce — as is all too often the case — or the bread.

Those pasta lovers, the Italians, know how to sauce a pasta well, which means lightly, and since they often consume it as a first course, they see no need for bread. And they know how to eat pasta properly too — with all the relish that this wonderfully varied, yet amazingly simple, food inspires.

How to Cook Pasta

Pasta is easy to cook; yet all too often it emerges soggy and sticky. Only a few steps need be followed to ensure perfectly cooked pasta every time.

☐ Use a big pot and lots of water. As the often repeated expression has it, pasta loves to swim.

☐ Let the water come to a full boil, then add the salt.

☐ With the water at a full boil, drop in the pasta, a few handfuls at a time; stir it to keep it from sticking.

Cover the pot so the water can come back to the boil quickly. Then uncover the pot to prevent boiling over, and adjust the heat to maintain a rolling boil.

☐ Begin timing the pasta once the water has resumed boiling. Test for doneness by biting into a piece of the pasta: When the pasta is *al dente* — that is, just right to the tooth, deliciously chewy without a floury taste — it is ready. Logic dictates that pastas of different thicknesses will take varying times to cook and that fresh pasta, with its higher moisture content, will cook faster than dried. How long a box of pasta has been on the grocer's shelf or on your own can matter too; the older the pasta, the drier it is likely to be and the longer therefore the cooking time. Manufacturers' instructions are not always reliable; the tooth test is safer.

☐ Drain the pasta at once. Do not rinse it unless the recipe says so (rinsing washes away nutrients).

☐ Sauce the pasta at once to keep it from adhering to itself and toss it well to distribute the sauce.

EDITOR'S NOTE: *All recipes for dried and fresh pastas in this book include recommended testing and cooking times. In most of the recipes, pasta is cooked according to the following proportions of water and salt:*

PASTA	WATER	SALT
4-6 oz.	2 qts.	1 tsp.
8-10 oz.	3 qts.	1½ tsp.
12-16 oz.	4 qts.	2 tsp.

1 *Nests of homemade pasta demonstrate the variety achieved when ingredients as diverse as cocoa, carrots, beets, tomato and spinach are added to dough.*

The Fun of Making Your Own

One of the pleasures of fresh pasta is making it yourself. You can experiment with a variety of shapes — perhaps even inventing your own — and you can add different flavors and colorful vegetable purées to the dough to please both palate and eye. Photographs on the following pages will show you how.

This section examines fresh pasta's many possibilities — as first course, entrée or side dish. The accompanying sauces, although created to go with a particular pasta, could as easily complement another fresh pasta or a dried pasta of a corresponding shape.

The difference between fresh and dried pasta lies not just in the freshness of the product but in the kinds of flour used. Most dried pastas are held together by the high gluten content of the semolina dough with which they are made. In this section pasta is prepared with unbleached all-purpose flour and eggs or with a mixture of finely milled semolina flour and unbleached all-purpose flour. One recipe also includes buckwheat flour, which, despite its name, contains no wheat at all; it consists instead of the ground seeds of the flowering buckwheat plant.

Recipes for fresh pasta doughs usually call for two eggs with one and one half cups of flour. In this section, to keep down the cholesterol in the dough, an egg white is substituted for one of the whole eggs. The recipes using semolina flour have no eggs at all.

Homemade pasta can be refrigerated for 24 hours when covered with plastic wrap, or the pasta can be frozen. It is rarely so good, however, as when it is eaten soon after being made. Since it has a relatively high moisture content, it need not be cooked long. And this has the advantage of allowing the ingredients with which some of the doughs have been colored — from spinach and tomatoes to carrots, beets and curry — to shine through undiminished.

Using a Pasta Machine

Making fresh pasta is greatly simplified when a good pasta machine takes over the job that otherwise would have to be done entirely by hand. You can quickly turn out noodles, or sheets of dough that may be cut and twisted into fancy shapes, such as bow ties, or used for ravioli and tortellini. Photographs on these two pages demonstrate the preparation of the basic dough.

The trick is to roll out the dough repeatedly: It should have a sheen and be satiny to the touch when ready. If the dough gets sticky, flour it well on both sides before running it through again.

You can cook the pasta immediately, or you can reserve all or part of it for later use. To dry it, hang the strands over a pasta drying rack or twist them loosely into ''nests'' on a lightly floured surface. When the pasta is thoroughly dry, store it in airtight containers.

To freeze fresh pasta, let it dry for 15 minutes or so. Then coil handfuls into nests of serving portion size and place these on a tray. Put the tray in the freezer for an hour; the stiffened pasta can then be stored in heavy-duty plastic bags in the freezer. To cook frozen pasta, put it directly into boiling water, without defrosting.

1 *ADDING EGG AND OIL TO FLOUR. Place the flour in a mixing bowl and make a well in the center. Drop one whole egg and one egg white into the well, then add the oil. (Alternatively, the dough can be prepared in a food processor following the directions in the basic pasta dough recipe on page 15.)*

2 *BLENDING THE INGREDIENTS. With a wooden spoon or a fork, break the egg yolk and mix it together with the egg whites and oil. Then broaden your strokes to incorporate the flour, and continue to mix until all of the liquid is absorbed and the dough can be gathered into a ball.*

3 *KNEADING BY HAND. Divide the dough into thirds. Cover two of the pieces with plastic wrap or a bowl to keep them from drying out. On a lightly floured work surface — preferably wood or marble — knead the third piece for several minutes. If the dough feels tough and inelastic, cover it and let it rest for 15 minutes.*

4 KNEADING BY MACHINE. *Flatten the dough to about one-inch thickness and lightly flour both sides. Set the knob for the pasta machine's smooth rollers on the widest setting. Pass the dough through the feeder, cranking the rollers with one hand and catching the dough with the other as it is extruded.*

5 FOLDING THE ROLLED DOUGH. *On a lightly floured surface, fold the piece into thirds and press it down to flatten it; then run it lengthwise through the machine once more. Repeat the process six to eight times, folding the dough into thirds each time. In the end, the surface should be smooth and satiny.*

6 REDUCING THE THICKNESS. *Adjust the control to the next smaller setting, and feed the entire sheet through the machine, without folding. Repeat the procedure, narrowing the setting each time, until the desired thickness is achieved — usually with the next-to-last setting. Flour the dough as necessary to prevent sticking, and support the sheet with your free hand to keep it as extended and flat as possible going into and coming out of the rollers.*

7 CUTTING NOODLES. *With a knife, cut the sheet of dough in half for easier manageability. Flour the strips lightly on both sides and allow them to rest for 10 to 15 minutes before handling them again. Then run one piece of dough at a time through the selected cutting rollers. Gently toss the noodles in flour and set them aside before cutting the next sheet. Repeat the procedures with the remaining sheets of dough.*

Mushroom-Stuffed Triangles

Serves 6 as an appetizer
Working (and total) time: about 50 minutes

Calories **267**
Protein **10g.**
Cholesterol **60mg.**
Total fat **8g.**
Saturated fat **3g.**
Sodium **291mg.**

basic or semolina pasta dough (recipes, page 15)
½ oz. dried wild mushrooms, preferably porcini, soaked for 20 minutes in enough boiling water to cover them
8 oz. fresh mushrooms, wiped clean and finely chopped
2 large shallots, finely chopped
3 garlic cloves, finely chopped
2 tbsp. balsamic vinegar, or 1 tbsp. red wine vinegar
¼ cup red wine
¼ tsp. salt
freshly ground black pepper
2 tbsp. fresh bread crumbs
2½ lb. ripe tomatoes, peeled, seeded and chopped, or 28 oz. unsalted canned whole tomatoes, drained and chopped
1 large onion, chopped
3 carrots (about ½ lb.), peeled and chopped
3 tbsp. heavy cream
⅓ cup freshly grated Parmesan cheese

To make the filling, drain the wild mushrooms, reserving their liquid. Finely chop them and transfer them to a large, heavy-bottomed skillet. Add the fresh mushrooms, shallots and two thirds of the garlic. Pour in the reserved mushroom-soaking liquid and bring the liquid to a boil over medium-high heat. Cook the mixture until nearly all the liquid has evaporated — about five minutes. Add the vinegar, wine, ⅛ teaspoon of the salt and a generous grinding of pepper. Continue cooking, stirring constantly, until all the liquid has boiled away — about three minutes more. Stir in the bread crumbs and set the mixture aside to cool.

To make the sauce, combine the tomatoes, onion, carrots, some pepper, the remaining garlic and the remaining ⅛ teaspoon of salt in a saucepan. Add ¼ cup of water and bring the liquid to a boil. Cook the mixture until the vegetables are soft and very little liquid remains — about 20 minutes. Purée the sauce in a food processor or blender and return it to the pan. Stir in the cream and set the pan aside.

Meanwhile, prepare the triangles. First divide the

pasta dough into four portions. Cover three of the portions with plastic wrap or an inverted bowl to keep them from drying out. Roll out the fourth portion to form a long strip about 5 inches wide and less than 1/16 inch thick (technique, pages 12-13). Cut across the dough at 5-inch intervals to form squares, then cut each of the squares into four smaller ones.

Mound about 1 teaspoon of the filling in the center of a square. Moisten the edges of two adjacent sides of the square. Fold the moistened edges over the filling to form a triangle, and press the edges closed. Repeat the process with the remaining dough and filling.

Add the pasta triangles to 3 quarts of boiling water with 1½ teaspoons of salt. Start testing the triangles after one minute and cook them until they are al dente.

Reheat the sauce over medium-high heat; if the sauce is too thick to pour easily, add one or two tablespoons of the pasta-cooking water. Drain the triangles and transfer them to a serving dish, then pour the warmed sauce over them. Serve immediately; pass the Parmesan cheese separately.

Basic Pasta Dough

Serves 4

Calories **211**	1½ to 1¾ cups unbleached all-purpose flour
Protein **7g.**	
Cholesterol **69mg.**	1 egg
Total fat **5g.**	1 egg white
Saturated fat **1g.**	1 tbsp. safflower oil
Sodium **31mg.**	

To prepare the dough in a food processor, put 1½ cups of the flour, the egg, egg white and oil in the bowl of the machine and process the mixture for about 30 seconds. If the mixture forms a ball immediately and is wet to the touch, mix in flour by the tablespoon until the dough feels soft but not sticky. If the mixture does not form a ball, try pinching it together with your fingers. If it is still too dry to work with, blend in water by the teaspoon until the dough just forms a ball. If you have a pasta machine, the dough may be immediately kneaded and rolled out (technique, pages 12-13).

To prepare the dough by hand, put 1½ cups of the flour into a mixing bowl and make a well in the center. Add the egg, egg white and oil to the well and stir them with a fork or wooden spoon, gradually mixing in the flour. Transfer the dough to a lightly floured surface and knead it for a few minutes. The dough should come cleanly away from the surface; if it is too wet, add flour by the tablespoon until the dough is no longer sticky. If the dough is too dry and crumbly to work with, add water by the teaspoon until it is pliable. Continue kneading the dough until it is smooth and elas-

tic — about 10 minutes; alternatively knead the dough in a pasta machine (technique, pages 12-13).

If you are not using a pasta machine, wrap the dough in wax paper or plastic wrap and let it rest for 15 minutes before rolling it out.

EDITOR'S NOTE: In a traditional pasta dough, two eggs are used with 1½ cups of flour. Here, to reduce the amount of cholesterol in the dough, an egg white has been substituted for one of the whole eggs.

Semolina Pasta Dough

Serves 4

Calories **210**	1 cup unbleached all-purpose flour
Protein **7g.**	
Cholesterol **0mg.**	1 cup semolina flour
Total fat **1g.**	
Saturated fat **0g.**	
Sodium **1mg.**	

To prepare the dough in a food processor, first blend the flours together, then gradually mix in up to ½ cup of water until the mixture just forms a ball. If the mixture is wet to the touch, blend in flour by the tablespoon until the dough feels soft but not sticky. If the mixture does not form a ball, try pinching it together with your fingers. If it is still too dry to work with, blend in water by the teaspoon until the dough just forms a ball. If you have a pasta machine, the dough may be immediately kneaded and rolled out (technique, pages 12-13).

To prepare the dough by hand, blend the flours in a bowl and make a well in the center. With a fork or a wooden spoon, gradually mix in up to ½ cup of water until the dough can be pressed together into a solid ball. Transfer the dough to a lightly floured surface and knead it for a few minutes. The dough should come cleanly away from the surface; if it is too wet, incorporate flour a tablespoon at a time until the dough is no longer sticky. If the dough feels dry and crumbly, incorporate water by the teaspoon until it is pliable. Continue kneading until the dough is smooth and elastic — about 10 minutes; alternatively, knead the dough in a pasta machine (technique, pages 12-13).

If you are not using a pasta machine, wrap the dough in wax paper or plastic wrap and let it rest for 15 minutes before rolling it out.

Fettuccine with Swordfish and Roasted Red Pepper

Serves 4
Working (and total) time: about 1 hour

Calories **376**
Protein **24g.**
Cholesterol **101mg.**
Total fat **15g.**
Saturated fat **2g.**
Sodium **217mg.**

basic pasta dough (recipe, page 15)
12 oz. swordfish steak, trimmed and cut into ½-inch cubes
2 garlic cloves, finely chopped
1 tbsp. fresh lemon juice
2 tbsp. virgin olive oil
1 red pepper
2 tbsp. chopped fresh parsley

In an ovenproof baking dish, combine the swordfish cubes, garlic, lemon juice and 1 tablespoon of the oil. Toss well, cover, and let the mixture marinate in the refrigerator for at least 30 minutes.

Roll out the dough and cut it into fettuccine *(technique, pages 12-13)*. Set the pasta aside while you prepare the swordfish and red pepper.

In a preheated broiler, roast the red pepper about 2 inches below the heat source, turning the pepper from time to time until it is charred on all sides. Transfer the pepper to a bowl and cover the bowl with plastic wrap, or put the pepper in a paper bag and fold it shut; the trapped steam will loosen the skin. Peel, seed and derib the pepper, holding it over the bowl to catch any juice. Cut the pepper into thin strips and strain the juice to remove any seeds. Set the strips and juice aside.

Set the oven temperature at 400° F. Bake the swordfish cubes in their marinade until they are cooked through — six to eight minutes.

Meanwhile, add the fettuccine to 3 quarts of boiling water with 1½ teaspoons of salt. Start testing the pasta after one minute and cook it until it is *al dente*. Drain

the pasta and transfer it to a large bowl. Add the remaining tablespoon of oil, the red pepper and juice, and the parsley; toss well. Add the swordfish and its cooking liquid, toss gently, and serve at once.

Tagliarini with Shrimp and Scallops

Serves 8
Working (and total) time: about 45 minutes

Calories **378**
Protein **23g.**
Cholesterol **154mg.**
Total fat **12g.**
Saturated fat **3g.**
Sodium **478mg.**

basic pasta dough (recipe, page 15)
spinach pasta dough (recipe, page 29)
1 lb. sea scallops
2 tbsp. unsalted butter
3 tbsp. finely chopped shallot
1 lb. large shrimp, shelled and deveined, the shells reserved
1 cup dry vermouth
1 small bay leaf
2 tbsp. safflower oil
2 tbsp. cut fresh chives
¼ tsp. salt
white pepper

Roll out the pasta doughs and cut them into tagliarini *(technique, pages 12-13)*. Set the tagliarini aside while you prepare the shrimp-and-scallop sauce.

Pull off and reserve the firm, small muscle, if there is one, from the side of each scallop. Rinse the scallops, pat them dry, and set them aside. Melt the butter in a heavy-bottomed saucepan over medium heat. Stir in the shallots and cook them until they are translucent — about two minutes. Add the reserved shrimp shells and any reserved side muscles from the scallops; cook, stirring, for one minute. Pour in the vermouth and simmer the mixture for one minute more.

Add the bay leaf and 1½ cups of water to the saucepan. Bring the liquid to a boil. Reduce the heat and simmer the liquid until it is reduced by about half — 10 to 12 minutes. Set the pan aside.

To prepare the seafood, heat the oil in a large, deep, heavy-bottomed skillet over medium-high heat. Add the shrimp and scallops, and sauté them for one and a half to two minutes, turning the pieces frequently with a spoon. Push the seafood to one side of the skillet and strain the liquid from the saucepan into the skillet. Set the skillet aside.

Add the tagliarini to 6 quarts of boiling water with 3 teaspoons of salt. Start testing the tagliarini after one minute and cook it until it is *al dente*. Drain the pasta and add it to the skillet with the seafood. Season with the chives, salt and some pepper, and toss gently to distribute the shrimp and scallops through the pasta. Cover the skillet and place it over medium heat to warm the mixture thoroughly — about one minute. Serve the tagliarini at once.

Parsley Stuffed
Mini-Ravioli

Serves 6
Working (and total) time: about 1 hour

Calories **217**
Protein **12g.**
Cholesterol **11mg.**
Total fat **4g.**
Saturated fat **2g.**
Sodium **329mg.**

semolina pasta dough (recipe, page 15)
½ cup part-skim ricotta cheese
½ cup low-fat cottage cheese
2 cups tightly packed parsley leaves, finely chopped
¼ cup freshly grated Parmesan cheese
¼ tsp. grated nutmeg
⅛ tsp. salt
freshly ground black pepper
½ cup skim milk

To prepare the filling, work the ricotta and cottage cheese through a sieve into a bowl. Stir in the parsley, Parmesan cheese, nutmeg, salt and some pepper. Set the mixture aside.

Roll out the dough. Then, following the steps shown on page 18, form it into ravioli that are each about 1½ inches square with ½ teaspoon of filling inside. Use only about half of the filling to stuff the squares.

To make the sauce, put the remaining filling in a pan over medium-high heat and stir in the milk. Cook the sauce until it is hot but not boiling — about five minutes. Keep the sauce warm while you cook the ravioli.

Add the ravioli to 3 quarts of boiling water with 1½ teaspoons of salt. Start testing the ravioli after one minute and cook them until they are *al dente,* then drain them. Pour the sauce over the ravioli and serve the dish immediately.

Making Ravioli

1 ADDING THE FILLING. *Spread the rolled dough sheet on a lightly floured surface. Place dollops of the filling on half of the sheet, taking care to space them evenly, about an inch apart.*

2 COVERING THE FILLING. *Brush the other half of the sheet lightly with water. Then fold it gently over the mounds of filling, matching the edges as closely as possible.*

3 CUTTING THE RAVIOLI. *Starting from the folded edge, use your fingers or the side of your hand to force out the air between the mounds of filling and to seal the dough. Then cut out the ravioli with a fluted pastry wheel.*

Pressed-Leaf Ravioli in Shallot Butter

Serves 6 as a side dish or first course
Working (and total) time: about 45 minutes

Calories **177**
Protein **5g.**
Cholesterol **56mg.**
Total fat **8g.**
Saturated fat **3g.**
Sodium **112mg.**

basic pasta dough or basic semolina dough (recipe, page 15)
½ cup combined Italian parsley, dill and celery leaves, the stems removed
2 tbsp. unsalted butter
1 tbsp. finely chopped shallot
¼ tsp. salt
freshly ground black pepper

Divide the dough into three pieces. Cover two of the pieces with plastic wrap or an inverted bowl to keep them from drying out, and roll out the third piece into a sheet about ¹⁄₁₆ inch thick *(technique, pages 12-13)*.

Place the pasta sheet on a lightly floured surface. Distribute one third of the leaves over half of the sheet so that they are about ½ inch apart. Carefully flatten each leaf in place. Lightly brush the uncovered half of the sheet with water and fold it over the leaves as shown below. Press the dough down firmly to seal the leaves in, forcing out any air bubbles.

Pass the folded sheet through the pasta machine to obtain a thickness of ¹⁄₁₆ inch. With a large, sharp chef's knife, cut the sheet into 2-inch squares. Set the squares aside and repeat the process with the remaining dough and leaves.

Melt the butter in a large, heavy-bottomed skillet over medium-high heat. Add the shallot and salt, and sauté the shallot until it turns translucent — about two minutes. Remove the pan from the heat.

Add the ravioli to 3 quarts of boiling water with 1½ teaspoons of salt. Start testing the ravioli after two minutes and cook them until they are *al dente*. Drain the ravioli and add them to the skillet with the shallot butter. Shake the pan gently to coat the pasta with the butter. Sprinkle on some pepper and serve hot.

EDITOR'S NOTE: *These ravioli make an excellent accompaniment to grilled lamb or veal chops. They may also be served without their sauce in a clear consommé.*

stirring once after four minutes, until all of the liquid is absorbed and the buckwheat groats are tender — about six minutes.

Meanwhile, drop the bow ties into 2 quarts of boiling water with 1 teaspoon of salt. Start testing the bow ties after one minute and cook them until they are *al dente*. Drain the bow ties and add them to the buckwheat mixture. Stir gently and serve hot.

EDITOR'S NOTE: *To intensify the flavors of the dish, prepare it a day in advance and refrigerate it. Reheat it in a shallow baking dish in a preheated 350° F. oven for 10 minutes, or microwave it on high for 90 seconds.*

Bow Ties with Buckwheat and Onions

Serves 4
Working (and total) time: about 45 minutes

Calories **211**
Protein **6g.**
Cholesterol **16mg.**
Total fat **7g.**
Saturated fat **4g.**
Sodium **262mg.**

semolina pasta dough (recipe, page 15, but halve the ingredients)
2 tbsp. unsalted butter
½ cup chopped onion
freshly ground black pepper
½ cup toasted cracked buckwheat groats (kasha)
1 egg white
¼ tsp. salt
¾ cup unsalted chicken stock

Cut the dough in half; cover one of the halves with plastic wrap or an inverted bowl to keep it moist. Roll out the other half into a long rectangle about ¹⁄₁₆ inch thick *(technique, pages 12-13)*. Following the steps demonstrated at right, cut the rectangle into strips and form the strips into bow ties. Repeat the process to fashion bow ties from the other piece of dough.

Melt the butter in a saucepan over medium heat. Add the onion and some pepper; cook for five minutes, stirring occasionally. Meanwhile, put the buckwheat groats in a bowl with the egg white and blend well, then add the mixture to the saucepan. Increase the heat to high and cook, stirring constantly with a fork, until the mixture is light and fluffy — three to four minutes. Add the salt and stock, then reduce the heat to low. Cover the pan tightly; simmer the mixture,

Shaping Bow Ties

1 CUTTING OUT THE TIES. *With a fluted pastry wheel or a knife, trim the edges of the rolled dough sheet on a flour-dusted surface. Divide the sheet down the middle. Then cut the strips into one-inch widths.*

2 TYING THE "KNOT." *Separate the pieces. Pinch the center of each between your thumb and forefinger to form bows, holding down the "knot" with the index finger of your other hand.*

Butternut Agnolotti

Serves 6 as a side dish or appetizer
Working time: about 30 minutes
Total time: about 1 hour and 15 minutes

Calories **335**
Protein **9g.**
Cholesterol **56mg.**
Total fat **12g.**
Saturated fat **3g.**
Sodium **324mg.**

basic pasta dough (recipe, page 15)
1 butternut squash (about 1 lb.), halved lengthwise and seeded
1½ cups unsalted chicken stock
2 tbsp. finely cut chives
⅓ cup finely chopped walnuts
1 tbsp. finely chopped fresh sage, or 1 tsp. ground sage
½ tsp. salt
¼ tsp. white pepper
2 tbsp. unsalted butter
2 tbsp. finely chopped shallots
2 tbsp. unbleached all-purpose flour
¼ cup cream sherry
¼ cup dark raisins
¼ cup golden raisins

To prepare the filling, preheat the oven to 400° F. Place the squash halves, cut sides up, on a lightly oiled baking sheet; bake them until they are soft — about one hour. Allow the squash to cool, then scoop out the pulp and put it in a food processor or blender along with 1 tablespoon of the stock. Purée the mixture and transfer it to a bowl. Stir in the chives, walnuts, sage, ¼ teaspoon of the salt and ⅛ teaspoon of the pepper.

Divide the dough into three pieces and set two of them aside, covered with an inverted bowl or plastic wrap. Roll out the third piece to a thickness of about ¹⁄₁₆ inch. Using a 3-inch-round cutter, cut the sheet of dough into about 12 circles. Then roll out and cut the other two pieces. Place 1 teaspoon of the filling near the center of each circle. Lightly brush the edges of the circles with water, then fold each circle in half, pressing gently on the edges to seal in the filling.

To make the sauce, melt the butter in a heavy-bottomed saucepan over medium heat. Add the shallots and cook them until they are translucent — about two minutes. Stir in the flour and cook, stirring, for one minute. Whisk in the remaining stock and the sherry, and continue cooking, whisking constantly, until the sauce thickens and turns smooth — about one minute more. Add the raisins, reduce the heat to low and simmer the sauce for three minutes. Season with the remaining ¼ teaspoon of salt and the remaining ⅛ teaspoon of pepper.

Cook the agnolotti in 3 quarts of gently boiling water with 1½ teaspoons of salt. (If necessary to avoid overcrowding, cook the pasta in several batches.) Start testing the agnolotti after two minutes and cook them until they are *al dente*. With a slotted spoon, transfer the agnolotti to a warmed, lightly buttered platter. Spoon the sauce over the agnolotti and serve warm.

Tortellini Stuffed with Veal

TORTELLINI WERE PRIZED IN THE MIDDLE AGES IN BOLOGNA,
ITALY'S CAPITAL OF FRESH PASTA COOKERY. ACCORDING
TO LEGEND, TORTELLINI WERE MODELED AFTER THE NAVEL OF
VENUS, THE GODDESS OF LOVE.

Serves 6
Working (and total) time: about 1 hour

Calories **311**
Protein **16g.**
Cholesterol **69mg.**
Total fat **13g.**
Saturated fat **4g.**
Sodium **358mg.**

basic pasta dough (recipe, page 15)
2 tbsp. virgin olive oil
1 onion, finely chopped
1 carrot, peeled and finely chopped
1 celery stalk, finely chopped
4 garlic cloves, very finely chopped
8 oz. ground veal
¼ tsp. salt
freshly ground black pepper
4 cups unsalted chicken stock
¼ cup Marsala
2 tbsp. tomato paste
¼ tsp. grated nutmeg
4 tbsp. freshly grated Parmesan cheese
2 tbsp. chopped parsley

Heat the oil in a large skillet over medium-high heat. Add the onion, carrot, celery and garlic, and cook them, stirring often, until the onion is translucent — about four minutes. Add the veal and continue cooking, turning the mixture frequently with a spatula or wooden spoon, until the veal is no longer pink — about five minutes. Add the salt and some pepper, 1 cup of the stock, the Marsala and the tomato paste. Cover the skillet, reduce the heat to medium, and cook for 30 minutes. Remove the skillet from the heat and stir in the nutmeg and two tablespoons of the cheese.

To prepare the pasta, roll out the dough *(technique, pages 12-13)* and form it into tortellini *(technique, page 23),* using 1 teaspoon of the veal mixture to fill each circle. Set the tortellini aside.

To make the sauce, reduce the remaining 3 cups of stock by one third over high heat — about five minutes. Stir in the parsley and keep the sauce warm.

Add the tortellini to 3 quarts of boiling water with 1½ teaspoons of salt. Start testing the tortellini when the water returns to a boil and cook them until they are *al dente* — about five minutes. Drain the pasta and transfer it to a bowl. Pour the sauce over the tortellini and pass the remaining 2 tablespoons of Parmesan cheese separately.

Shaping Tortellini

1 *FILLING THE TORTELLINI. With a 2½- to 3-inch biscuit cutter, cut circles from the dough. Stack them or store them under a towel or a bowl to keep them from drying out. Place some filling on a circle, then moisten half of the circle's edge.*

2 *ENCLOSING THE FILLING. Fold the circle in half so that the moist and dry edges meet. Press the edges firmly shut to seal them.*

3 *JOINING THE ENDS. Curl the ends around the filling and pinch these together, moistening the inner surfaces, if necessary, to make them stick. Repeat the steps with the remaining circles.*

Tortellini Stuffed with Escargots

Serves 2 (about 24 tortellini)
Working (and total) time: about 45 minutes

Calories **371**
Protein **16g.**
Cholesterol **121mg.**
Total fat **13g.**
Saturated fat **8g.**
Sodium **350mg.**

basic semolina pasta dough (recipe, page 15, but halve the ingredients)
1 tbsp. unsalted butter
1 tbsp. very finely chopped onion
1 garlic clove, very finely chopped
12 giant snails (escargots), drained and cut in half (about 4 oz.)
2 tsp. fresh lemon juice
½ tsp. chopped fresh thyme, or ¼ tsp. dried thyme leaves
⅛ tsp. salt
freshly ground black pepper
3 tbsp. finely chopped fresh parsley
¼ cup light cream

Melt the butter in a heavy-bottomed skillet over medium heat. Add the onion and garlic and cook them, stirring often, for three minutes. Add the snails, lemon juice, thyme, salt and some pepper; cook for three minutes more, stirring frequently. Stir in the parsley and remove the skillet from the heat. Transfer the snails to a small dish and refrigerate them. Stir the cream into the skillet and set the skillet aside.

Cut the dough into two pieces. Cover one of them with plastic wrap or an inverted bowl to keep it moist. Roll out the other piece into a sheet about ¹⁄₁₆ inch thick *(technique, pages 12-13)*. With a 3-inch-round cutter, cut the sheet into 12 circles. Place a snail half slightly off center on one of the dough circles. Form the round of dough into the shape of a tortellini as demonstrated above. Repeat the process with the remaining dough rounds and then with the other piece of dough.

Cook the tortellini in 3 quarts of boiling water with 1½ teaspoons of salt until they float to the top and are *al dente* — four to five minutes. Meanwhile, heat the sauce in the skillet. Drain the tortellini, toss them with the sauce, and serve immediately.

Fettuccine with Oysters, Spinach and Fennel

Serves 4
Working (and total) time: about 1 hour

Calories **418**
Protein **22g.**
Cholesterol **138mg.**
Total fat **14g.**
Saturated fat **5g.**
Sodium **276mg.**

basic pasta dough (recipe, page 15)
2 tbsp. unsalted butter
1 head of fennel, trimmed, cored and thinly sliced
4 scallions, trimmed and thinly sliced
1 lb. fresh spinach, washed and stemmed
1 shallot, finely chopped
½ cup dry white wine
1 tbsp. chopped fresh tarragon, or 1 tsp. dried tarragon
16 oysters (about 1 pint), shucked and drained, the liquid reserved (about ⅔ cup)

Roll out the dough and cut it into fettuccine *(technique, pages 12-13)*. Set the fettuccine aside while you prepare the sauce.

In a heavy-bottomed skillet over medium-low heat, melt 1 tablespoon of the butter. Add the fennel and scallions, cover the pan, and cook the vegetables until they are tender — about 10 minutes.

Meanwhile, blanch the spinach in 3 quarts of boiling water for 40 seconds. Drain the spinach and refresh it under cold water. Squeeze the spinach dry and separate the leaves. When the fennel and scallions finish cooking, add the spinach leaves to the skillet and remove it from the heat.

In a small saucepan, combine the shallot, wine and half of the tarragon. Cook the mixture over medium-high heat until the liquid is reduced by half — about five minutes. Add the reserved oyster liquid and bring it to a simmer — about three minutes. Add the oysters to the pan and cook them just until their edges begin to curl — about two minutes. Reduce the heat to low to keep the oysters warm.

Cook the fettuccine in 3 quarts of boiling water with 1½ teaspoons of salt. Start testing the pasta after one minute and cook it until it is *al dente*. Drain the pasta and transfer it to a large bowl. Swirl the remaining tablespoon of butter into the oyster sauce and combine the sauce with the pasta. Reheat the vegetables in the skillet and stir in the remaining tarragon, then add the vegetables to the pasta and oyster sauce. Toss well and serve immediately.

Beet Ravioli in Sour-Cream-and-Chive Sauce

Serves 6
Working time: about 1 hour
Total time: about 2 hours

Calories **248**	
Protein **8g.**	*1 lb. fresh beets, washed and trimmed, a 2-inch stem left on each beet, or 1 lb. canned beets, drained*
Cholesterol **54mg.**	*¼ cup bulgur*
Total fat **10g.**	*1 tbsp. white vinegar*
Saturated fat **3g.**	*1½ tbsp. horseradish*
Sodium **302mg.**	*¼ tsp. salt*
	freshly ground black pepper
	1½ to 1¾ cups unbleached all-purpose flour
	1 egg
	1 egg white
	1 tbsp. safflower oil
	Sour-cream-and-chive sauce
	1 tbsp. virgin olive oil
	1 small onion, finely chopped
	½ cup sour cream
	½ cup plain low-fat yogurt
	2 tbsp. finely cut fresh chives

If you are using fresh beets, preheat the oven to 400° F. Tightly wrap each beet in aluminum foil, with the foil's dull side out. Bake the beets until they are tender — about one hour. (The beets may be cooked up to 24 hours ahead of time.)

Meanwhile, put the bulgur in a bowl and pour ½ cup of boiling water over it. Let the bulgur stand for at least 30 minutes.

Peel the beets when they are cool enough to handle. Finely chop half of the beets and add them to the bulgur. Stir in the vinegar, ½ tablespoon of the horseradish, ⅛ teaspoon of the salt and a generous grinding of pepper. Set the mixture aside.

Cut a 1-inch-thick slice from one of the remaining beets and purée it in a blender or food mill — it will yield about 2 tablespoons of purée. Cut the rest of the beets into julienne and set them aside in a warm place.

To prepare the pasta dough in a food processor, put 1½ cups of the flour, the egg, egg white, oil and beet purée in the bowl of the machine and process the mixture for about 30 seconds. If the mixture forms a ball immediately and is wet to the touch, mix in flour by the tablespoon until the dough feels soft but not sticky. If the mixture does not form a ball, try pinching it together with your fingers. If it is still too dry to work ▶

with, blend in water by the teaspoon until the dough just forms a ball. If you have a pasta machine, the dough may be immediately kneaded and rolled out *(technique, pages 12-13)*.

To prepare the dough by hand, put 1½ cups of the flour in a mixing bowl and make a well in the center. Add the egg, egg white, oil and beet purée to the well, and stir them with a fork or wooden spoon, gradually mixing in the flour. Transfer the dough to a lightly floured surface and knead it for a few minutes. The dough should come cleanly away from the surface; if it is too wet, add flour by the tablespoon until the dough is no longer sticky. If the dough is too dry and crumbly to work with, add water by the teaspoon until the mixture is pliable. Continue kneading the dough until it is smooth and elastic — about 10 minutes; alternatively, knead the dough with a pasta machine *(technique, pages 12-13)*.

If you are not using a pasta machine, wrap the dough in wax paper or plastic wrap and let it rest for 15 minutes before rolling it out.

Form the dough into ravioli *(technique, page 18)*, filling the ravioli with the beet-and-bulgur mixture.

To make the sauce, heat the oil in a heavy-bottomed saucepan over medium-high heat. Add the onion and cook it until it is translucent — about four minutes. Reduce the heat to low. Stir in the sour cream and yogurt and heat them through; do not let the sauce boil or the yogurt will separate. Remove the sauce from the heat, then stir in the chives, the remaining ⅛ teaspoon of salt and the remaining tablespoon of horseradish; keep the sauce warm.

Add the ravioli to 3 quarts of boiling water with 1½ teaspoons of salt. Start testing the ravioli after three minutes and cook them until they are *al dente*. Drain the pasta, transfer it to a serving dish, and top it with the sauce. Distribute the julienned beets around the ravioli and serve the dish immediately.

Calories **315**
Protein **10g.**
Cholesterol **31mg.**
Total fat **13g.**
Saturated fat **7g.**
Sodium **274mg.**

Spinach Orecchiette Tossed with Cauliflower

THIS RUSTIC ITALIAN PASTA, AFFECTIONATELY CALLED "LITTLE EARS," DOES NOT REQUIRE THE USE OF A PASTA MACHINE.

Serves 4
Working (and total) time: about 1 hour and 15 minutes

5 oz. frozen spinach, defrosted, or ½ lb. fresh spinach, washed, stemmed and blanched in boiling water for one minute
¾ cup unbleached all-purpose flour
¾ cup semolina flour
4 tbsp. unsalted butter
1 small cauliflower (about 1½ lb.), cored and cut into small florets
¼ tsp. salt
1 tsp. fresh thyme, or ¼ tsp. dried thyme leaves
freshly ground black pepper
2 garlic cloves, finely chopped
3 tbsp. dry bread crumbs
1 tsp. chopped fresh sage, or ¼ tsp. ground sage

To prepare the pasta dough, squeeze the spinach dry, then chop it finely. Put the flours together in a large mixing bowl. Add the spinach, then use your hands to combine it with the flours, rubbing the mixture between your fingertips to mix it evenly. Press the dough into a ball. If the dough is too dry to hold together, add a tablespoon of water and mix again. Add more water a teaspoon at a time, if necessary; the dough should be fairly dry. Knead the dough until it is smooth and elastic — about 10 minutes. Cut the dough into four pieces, then cover three of the pieces with plastic wrap or an inverted bowl to keep them from drying out.

Molding Orecchiette

DIMPLING THE DOUGH. After forming a dough roll and cutting off rounds, flatten the pieces. Place a round in the palm of one hand, and indent the center by pressing the thumb or forefinger of your other hand into it. Repeat with the other rounds.

To form the orecchiette, roll the remaining piece of dough into the shape of a rope about ½ inch in diameter. With a sharp knife, slice off rounds about ⅛ inch thick. Dip the rounds in flour to coat them lightly and make them easier to work with. Put a round in your palm and indent the center with a finger of your other hand, flattening the round to a diameter of about 1 inch. Repeat the process with the remaining rounds of dough and then with the three reserved pieces.

Add the orecchiette to 3 quarts of boiling water with 1½ teaspoons of salt. Start testing after 20 minutes and cook them until they are *al dente.*

While the pasta is cooking, heat 2 tablespoons of the butter in a large, heavy-bottomed skillet over medium-high heat. When the foam subsides, add the cauliflower florets and sauté them for four minutes, stirring once. Season the cauliflower with the salt, thyme and some pepper. Reduce the heat to medium and continue cooking the cauliflower until it turns golden brown all over — six to eight minutes more. Transfer the florets to a large, warmed bowl.

Reduce the heat under the skillet to low. Add the remaining 2 tablespoons of butter and the garlic, and cook for 15 seconds. Add the bread crumbs, sage and some more pepper; cook the bread crumbs, stirring frequently, until they are a crisp golden brown — about four minutes.

Drain the pasta, transfer it to the bowl with the cauliflower, and toss well. Scatter the bread crumbs over the top just before serving the dish.

Tomato Fettuccine
with Artichokes and Mint

Serves 4
Working (and total) time: about 40 minutes

Calories **308**
Protein **9g.**
Cholesterol **69mg.**
Total fat **12g.**
Saturated fat **2g.**
Sodium **430mg.**

Tomato pasta dough
1 egg
1 egg white
3 tbsp. tomato paste
1 tbsp. virgin olive oil
1½ to 1¾ cups unbleached all-purpose flour

Artichoke-and-mint sauce
6 artichokes
juice of 1 lemon
½ tsp. salt
freshly ground black pepper
4 garlic cloves, finely chopped
2 tbsp. chopped fresh mint or basil
2 tbsp. virgin olive oil

To prepare the dough in a food processor, blend the egg, egg white, tomato paste and oil for five seconds. Add 1½ cups of the flour and process the mixture for about 30 seconds. If the mixture forms a ball right away and is wet to the touch, mix in flour by the tablespoon until the dough feels soft but not sticky. If the mixture does not form a ball, try pressing it into a ball with your hands. If the dough is still too dry to work with, blend in water by the teaspoon until the mixture can be formed into a ball. If you have a pasta machine, the dough may be immediately kneaded and rolled out *(technique, pages 12-13)*.

To prepare the dough by hand, put 1½ cups of the flour in a mixing bowl and make a well in the center. Add the egg, egg white, tomato paste and oil to the well and mix them, gradually incorporating the flour. Transfer the dough to a lightly floured surface and knead it for a few minutes. The dough should come cleanly away from the surface; if it is too wet, add flour by the tablespoon until the dough is no longer sticky. If the dough is too dry and crumbly to work with, add water by the teaspoon until it is pliable. Continue kneading the dough until it is smooth and elastic — about 10 minutes; alternatively, knead the dough in a pasta machine *(technique, pages 12-13)*.

If you are not using a pasta machine, wrap the dough in wax paper or plastic wrap and let it rest for 15 minutes before rolling it out.

After the dough is rolled out, cut it into fettuccine *(technique, page 13)*. Set the strips aside.

To prepare the artichokes, pour enough water into a large, nonreactive skillet to fill it about 1 inch deep. Add the lemon juice, salt, some pepper and the garlic. Break or cut off the stem of an artichoke. Snap off and discard the leaves, starting at the base and continuing until you reach the pale yellow leaves of the core. Using a large, sharp knife, cut through the base of the pale yellow leaves, then discard them. With a paring knife, trim away any purple leaves and the fuzzy choke, then cut the artichoke bottom into quarters. Cut each quarter into four wedges and drop them into the water in the skillet. Repeat with the remaining artichokes.

Place the skillet over medium-high heat and bring the liquid to a boil. Reduce the heat and simmer the liquid until only ¼ cup remains and the artichokes are tender — about 15 minutes.

Meanwhile, bring 3 quarts of water to a boil with 1½ teaspoons of salt. Add the fettuccine to the boiling water. Start testing after two minutes and cook the pasta until it is *al dente*. Drain the fettuccine and add it to the skillet with the artichokes. Add the mint or basil and the olive oil, toss well, and serve.

Spinach Pasta Dough

Serves 4

Calories **216**
Protein **8g.**
Cholesterol **69mg.**
Total fat **5g.**
Saturated fat **1g.**
Sodium **42mg.**

1½ to 1¾ cups unbleached all-purpose flour
3 tbsp. finely chopped spinach (about 5 oz. frozen spinach, defrosted, or ½ lb. fresh spinach, washed, stemmed and blanched in boiling water for one minute)
1 egg
1 egg white
1 tbsp. safflower oil

To prepare the dough in a food processor, purée the spinach with the egg, egg white and oil for five seconds. Add 1½ cups of the flour and process the mixture for about 30 seconds. If the mixture forms a ball right away and is wet to the touch, mix in flour by the tablespoon until the dough feels soft but not sticky. If the mixture does not form a ball, try pinching it together with your fingers. If it is still too dry to work with, blend in water by the teaspoon until it can be formed into a ball. If you have a pasta machine, the dough may be immediately kneaded and rolled out *(technique, pages 12-13)*.

To prepare the dough by hand, put 1½ cups of the flour in a mixing bowl and make a well in the center. Add the spinach, egg, egg white and oil to the well and mix them, gradually incorporating the flour. Transfer the dough to a lightly floured surface and knead it for a few minutes. The dough should come cleanly away from the surface; if it is too wet, add flour by the tablespoon until the dough is no longer sticky. If the dough is too dry and crumbly to work with, add water by the teaspoon until it is pliable. Continue kneading the dough until it is smooth and elastic — about 10 minutes; alternatively, knead the dough in a pasta machine *(technique, pages 12-13)*.

If you are not using a pasta machine, wrap the dough in wax paper or plastic wrap and let it rest for 15 minutes before rolling it out.

Crab Pillows

Serves 4
Working (and total) time: about 1 hour and 15 minutes

Calories **348**
Protein **24g.**
Cholesterol **143mg.**
Total fat **10g.**
Saturated fat **3g.**
Sodium **326mg.**

spinach pasta dough (recipe, page 29)
¾ lb. crab meat, all bits of shell removed and discarded
6 scallions, green and white parts separated and thinly sliced
1½ tsp. finely chopped fresh ginger
10 drops hot red-pepper sauce
1½ lb. ripe tomatoes, peeled and seeded, or 14 oz. unsalted canned whole tomatoes, drained
1 tbsp. white wine vinegar
1 garlic clove, finely chopped
⅛ tsp. cayenne pepper
2 tbsp. heavy cream

To make the filling, combine the crab meat, the green scallion parts, the ginger and the hot red-pepper sauce. Refrigerate the mixture.

To prepare the sauce, first purée the tomatoes in a food processor or blender. Put the purée in a saucepan. Add the vinegar, garlic, cayenne pepper and the white scallion parts, and bring the liquid to a boil. Reduce the heat to low and simmer the sauce for 10 minutes. Set the pan aside.

Divide the pasta dough into two pieces. Roll out each piece into a strip approximately 1/16 inch thick and 4 inches wide and place the strips on a lightly floured surface *(technique, page 13)*. Cut the strips into 5-inch lengths to form 4-by-5-inch rectangles. Spread about 2 tablespoons of the crab filling on one half of each rectangle, leaving an uncovered border about ½ inch wide. Moisten the edges of the rectangles lightly with your fingers, then fold the dough over the filling to form smaller rectangles that are about 2½ inches by 4 inches. Press the edges firmly to seal in the filling. With a fluted pastry wheel or a knife, trim the edges. Use the dull side of a knife to press down along each of the three sealed edges; this leaves a decorative indentation and reinforces the seal.

Cook the pillows in 4 quarts of boiling water with 2 teaspoons of salt for five minutes, gently turning the pillows over with a slotted spoon halfway through the cooking. While the pillows are cooking, warm the sauce over low heat, then whisk in the cream. Spoon half the sauce onto a heated platter.

Remove the pillows from the boiling water with a slotted spoon, allowing most of the water to drain off. Arrange the pillows on the platter. Serve the remaining sauce separately.

Spinach Fettuccine with Endive and Bacon

Serves 6 as an appetizer
Working (and total) time: about 30 minutes

Calories **215**
Protein **8g.**
Cholesterol **50mg.**
Total fat **10g.**
Saturated fat **2g.**
Sodium **263mg.**

spinach pasta dough (recipe, page 29)
5 strips lean bacon, cut into ½-inch pieces
1½ tbsp. virgin olive oil
2 large Belgian endives (about ⅔ lb.), ends trimmed, the leaves cut diagonally into 1-inch strips and tossed with 1 tbsp. fresh lemon juice
⅛ tsp. salt
freshly ground black pepper

Roll out the dough and cut it into fettuccine *(technique, pages 12-13)*. Set the fettuccine aside on a lightly floured surface.

Meanwhile, cook the bacon pieces in a large, heavy-bottomed skillet over medium heat, stirring occasionally, until they are crisp — about eight minutes. Remove the pan from the heat; with a slotted spoon, transfer the bacon pieces to a paper towel to drain. Pour off all but about 2 tablespoons of the bacon fat from the skillet, and return the pan to the heat. Add the olive oil and the endive. Sauté the endive, stirring frequently, for two minutes, then sprinkle it with the salt and some pepper.

While the endive cooks, add the fettuccine to 3 quarts of boiling water with 1½ teaspoons of salt and cook it until it is *al dente* — about two minutes. Drain the pasta and add it to the endive in the skillet. Add the bacon pieces, toss well, and serve at once.

Agnolotti Filled with Turkey Mole

Serves 4 (about 36 agnolotti)
Working (and total) time: about 1 hour

Calories **444**
Protein **34g.**
Cholesterol **141mg.**
Total fat **14g.**
Saturated fat **4g.**
Sodium **371mg.**

Turkey filling
1½ lb. whole turkey leg, the thigh skinned and boned to yield 1 cup of meat, the drumstick, bone and remaining meat reserved for the sauce
1 tbsp. safflower oil
2 garlic cloves, finely chopped
1 onion, finely chopped
1 jalapeño pepper, seeded and finely chopped (caution, page 33)
¼ tsp. salt
2 tbsp. chopped cilantro
1 tbsp. grated semisweet chocolate

Cocoa pasta dough
1½ to 1¾ cups unbleached all-purpose flour
1½ tbsp. cocoa
1 egg
1 egg white

Cilantro sauce
2 ripe tomatoes, peeled, seeded and chopped
1 garlic clove, finely chopped
1 tbsp. fresh lemon juice
freshly ground black pepper
¾ cup cilantro leaves
1 scallion, thinly sliced

Reserve the cup of turkey thigh meat. Cut the meat from the drumstick, and put it into a saucepan together with the bones and any remaining thigh meat; pour in enough water to cover them by 1 inch. Cook over medium-high heat until the stock is reduced to ⅔ cup — 30 to 45 minutes.

Meanwhile, prepare the filling. Mince the reserved cup of turkey meat. Pour the oil into a large, heavy-bottomed skillet over low heat. Add the garlic, onion and jalapeño pepper. Cook, stirring frequently, for five minutes. Add the chopped turkey meat and salt, and stir the mixture until it is well blended and the turkey's color has begun to lighten — about one minute. Immediately transfer the filling to a bowl and stir in the cilantro and grated chocolate. Refrigerate the filling.

To make the cocoa pasta dough in a food processor, put 1½ cups of the flour, the cocoa, egg and egg white into the bowl and process for 30 seconds. If the mixture forms a ball immediately and is wet to the touch, mix in flour by the tablespoon until the dough feels soft but not sticky. If the mixture does not form a ball, try pinching it together with your fingers. If it is still too dry to work with, blend in water by the teaspoon until the dough just forms a ball. If you have a pasta machine,

the dough may be immediately kneaded and rolled out (technique, pages 12-13).

To prepare the dough by hand, mix the flour and cocoa in a bowl and make a well in the center. Add the egg and egg white, and stir them with a fork or a wooden spoon, gradually mixing in the flour. Transfer the dough to a lightly floured surface and knead it for a few minutes. The dough should come cleanly away from the surface; if it is too wet, add flour by the tablespoon until the dough is no longer sticky. If the dough is too dry and crumbly to work with, add water by the teaspoon until it is pliable. Continue kneading the dough until it is smooth and elastic — about 10 minutes; alternatively, knead the dough in a pasta machine (technique, pages 12-13).

If you are not using a pasta machine, wrap the dough in wax paper or plastic wrap and let it rest for 15 minutes before rolling it out.

Divide the dough into three pieces; set two of the pieces aside, covered with an inverted bowl or plastic wrap. Roll out the remaining piece into a sheet about ¹⁄₁₆ inch thick. Using a 3-inch-round cutter, cut the sheet into about 12 circles. Place 1 teaspoon of the filling slightly off center on each circle. Moisten the edges of the circles with water, then fold each circle in half, pressing firmly on the edges to seal in the filling. Repeat with the remaining two pieces of dough to make about 36 agnolotti.

To make the sauce, strain the reduced stock into a saucepan. Add the tomatoes, garlic, lemon juice and some pepper, and bring the liquid to a boil. Reduce the heat to low and simmer the mixture for three minutes. Remove the pan from the heat and stir in the cilantro and scallion.

Cook the agnolotti in 3 quarts of boiling water with 1½ teaspoons of salt, stirring once, until the agnolotti float to the top — about three minutes. (If necessary to avoid overcrowding, cook the pasta in several batches.) With a slotted spoon, remove the agnolotti and keep them warm. Spoon the sauce over them just before serving.

Chilies — A Cautionary Note

Both dried and fresh hot chilies should be handled with care. Their flesh and seeds contain volatile oils that can make skin tingle and cause eyes to burn. Rubber gloves offer protection — but the cook should still be careful not to touch the face, lips or eyes when working with chilies.

Soaking fresh chilies in cold, salted water for an hour will remove some of their fire. If canned chilies are substituted for fresh ones, they should be rinsed in cold water in order to eliminate as much of the brine used to preserve them as possible.

well in the center of the cornmeal mixture and pour the whisked eggs into the well. Stir the eggs, gradually incorporating the cornmeal mixture into them. When almost all of the dry ingredients are incorporated, add the olive oil and work it into the dough by hand.

Transfer the dough to a flour-dusted work surface and begin kneading it. If the dough is stiff and crumbly, add water, a teaspoon at a time; if it is too wet and sticky, gradually add flour, a tablespoon at a time, until the dough pulls away cleanly from the work surface and no longer sticks to your hands. Knead the dough until it is soft and pliable — 10 to 15 minutes. Wrap the dough in plastic wrap to keep it from drying out, then let it rest for 15 minutes to make it easier to roll out.

Dust the work surface with cornmeal. Remove the plastic wrap and roll the dough into a 2-foot-by-9-inch rectangle; cut it crosswise into ½-inch-wide strips.

To prepare the sauce, heat the safflower oil in a large, heavy-bottomed skillet over medium heat. Add the garlic and red chilies or crushed red pepper, and cook them, stirring frequently, until the garlic turns a light brown — about four minutes. Add the green pepper and salt, and cook for five minutes more. Stir in the tomato, vinegar and butter, and cook the mixture for an additional two minutes.

Add the dough strips to 3 quarts of boiling water with 1½ teaspoons of salt; cover the pan. When the water returns to a boil, cook the pasta for six minutes. Drain the noodles and add them to the skillet containing the sauce. Toss well and serve hot.

All-American Corn Pasta with Chilies and Tomato

Serves 4
Working (and total) time: about 1 hour

Calories **297**
Protein **8g.**
Cholesterol **76mg.**
Total fat **12g.**
Saturated fat **3g.**
Sodium **267mg.**

Corn pasta dough
¾ cup finely ground cornmeal
¾ cup bread flour
1 egg
1 egg white
1 tbsp. virgin olive oil

Hot chili and tomato sauce
1 tbsp. safflower oil
5 garlic cloves, peeled and thinly sliced
2 small dried red chilies, finely chopped (caution, page 33), or ½ tsp. crushed red pepper
1 green pepper, seeded, deribbed and chopped
¼ tsp. salt
1 large ripe tomato, peeled, seeded and finely chopped
1 tbsp. red wine vinegar
1 tbsp. unsalted butter

To make the pasta dough, mix the cornmeal and flour in a large bowl. In a small bowl, whisk together the egg, egg white and 3 tablespoons of water. Make a

Buckwheat Pasta in a Sauce of Green Peppercorns and Mustard

Serves 4
Working (and total) time: about 30 minutes

Calories **374**
Protein **13g.**
Cholesterol **76mg.**
Total fat **11g.**
Saturated fat **2g.**
Sodium **386mg.**

Buckwheat pasta dough
1½ cups unbleached all-purpose flour
½ cup buckwheat flour
1 egg
1 egg white
1 tbsp. safflower oil

Mustard-peppercorn sauce
1 tbsp. safflower oil
1 tbsp. finely chopped shallots
½ cup dry white wine
2 tsp. Dijon mustard
1 tbsp. green peppercorns, rinsed, drained and crushed
1½ cups low-fat milk
1 tomato, peeled, seeded and coarsely chopped
½ tsp. salt
parsley sprigs for garnish

To prepare the dough in a food processor, put the flours, egg, egg white and oil into the bowl of the machine and process the mixture for about 30 seconds. If the mixture forms a ball immediately and is wet to the touch, mix in flour by the tablespoon until the dough feels soft but not sticky. If the mixture does not form a ball, try pinching it together with your fingers. If it is still too dry to work with, blend in water by the teaspoon until the dough just forms a ball. Transfer the dough to a lightly floured surface and knead it for a few minutes. If you have a pasta machine, use it to complete the kneading and roll out the dough *(technique, pages 12-13)*.

To prepare the dough by hand, put the flours into a mixing bowl and make a well in the center. Add the egg, egg white and oil to the well and stir them with a fork or wooden spoon, gradually mixing in the flour. Transfer the dough to a lightly floured surface and knead it for a few minutes. The dough should come cleanly away from the surface; if it is too wet, add flour by the tablespoon until the dough is no longer sticky. If the dough is too dry and crumbly to work with, add water by the teaspoon until it is pliable. Continue

kneading the dough until it is smooth and elastic — about 10 minutes; alternatively, knead the dough by hand for a few minutes, then in a pasta machine *(technique, pages 12-13)*.

If you are not using a pasta machine, wrap the dough in wax paper or plastic wrap and let it rest for 15 minutes before rolling it out.

After the dough is rolled out, cut it into fettuccine *(technique, page 13)*.

To prepare the sauce, first heat the oil in a large, heavy-bottomed skillet over medium-high heat. Add the shallots and sauté them until they are translucent — about one minute. Add the white wine, mustard and peppercorns. Cook, stirring, until almost all the wine has evaporated. Add the milk, return the mixture to a simmer, and reduce the heat to medium low. Add the noodles and simmer them in the sauce until they are *al dente* — about three minutes. Stir in the chopped tomato and season the dish with the salt. Garnish with the parsley and serve immediately.

Pappardelle with Turkey Braised in Red Wine

PAPPARDELLE ARE BROAD ITALIAN NOODLES. CUTTING THEM WITH A FLUTED PASTRY WHEEL GIVES THEM THEIR CHARACTERISTIC ZIGZAG EDGES.

Serves 8
Working time: about 1 hour and 45 minutes
Total time: about 4 hours

Calories **418**
Protein **25g.**
Cholesterol **91mg.**
Total fat **10g.**
Saturated fat **3g.**
Sodium **240mg.**

Carrot pasta dough
½ lb. carrots, peeled and thinly sliced (about 2 cups)
1¾ to 2 cups unbleached all-purpose flour
1 egg
1 egg white
1 tbsp. safflower oil

Turkey sauce
¼ tsp. fresh thyme, or ⅛ tsp. dried thyme leaves
1 bay leaf
6 black peppercorns
1 clove
6 juniper berries, or 2 tbsp. gin
1 onion, thinly sliced
1 carrot, peeled and thinly sliced
1 celery stalk, trimmed and thinly sliced
3 garlic cloves, crushed
1 bottle (750 ml.) red wine, more if needed
¼ cup cognac
3 turkey drumsticks (about ¾ lb. each)
¼ cup all-purpose flour
1 tbsp. safflower oil
6 oz. mushrooms, wiped clean and quartered
2 cups pearl onions, peeled
¼ cup freshly grated Parmesan cheese

To make the turkey sauce, first prepare a turkey marinade: Wrap the thyme, bay leaf, peppercorns, clove and juniper berries if you are using them in a 4-inch-square piece of cheesecloth. In a large, nonreactive ovenproof casserole, combine the gin (if you are using it in place of the juniper berries), the onion, carrot, celery, garlic, the bundle of seasonings and the wine. Bring the mixture to a boil, then lower the heat and simmer it for 15 minutes. Set the casserole aside; when the marinade is cool, stir in the cognac. Put the drumsticks in the casserole. (There should be enough liquid to nearly cover the legs; if there is not, pour in more wine.) Allow the drumsticks to marinate in the refrigerator for at least two hours.

For the pasta dough, put the carrots in a saucepan over medium-high heat and pour in enough water to cover them. Bring the water to a boil and cook the carrots until they are tender — about seven minutes. Drain the carrots well and purée them, using a food processor, food mill or sieve. Return the purée to the saucepan and cook over medium heat, stirring constantly, to evaporate as much liquid as possible from the purée without scorching it — about three minutes. Set the purée aside.

If you are using a food processor to make the pasta dough, put 1¾ cups of the flour, the egg, egg white, carrot purée and oil in the bowl of the machine and process the mixture for about 30 seconds. If the mixture forms a ball immediately and is wet to the touch, mix in flour by the tablespoon until the dough feels soft but not sticky. If the mixture does not form a ball, try pinching it together with your fingers. If it is still too dry to work with, blend in water by the teaspoon until the dough just forms a ball. If you have a pasta machine, the dough may be immediately kneaded and rolled out (technique, pages 12-13).

To prepare the pasta dough by hand, put 1¾ cups of the flour into a mixing bowl and make a well in the center. Add the egg, egg white, carrot purée and oil to the well; stir them with a fork or wooden spoon, gradually mixing in the flour. Transfer the dough to a lightly floured surface and knead it for a few minutes. The dough should come cleanly away from the surface; if it is too wet, add flour by the tablespoon until the dough is no longer sticky. If the dough is too dry and crumbly to work with, add water by the teaspoon until it is pliable. Continue kneading the dough until it is smooth and elastic — about 10 minutes; alternatively, knead and roll out the dough in a pasta machine (technique, pages 12-13).

If you are not using a pasta machine, wrap the dough in wax paper or plastic wrap and let it rest for 15 minutes before rolling it out.

Cut the sheet of dough into pappardelle, using a fluted pastry wheel or a knife to form strips ½ to ¾ inch wide. (Alternatively, cut the dough into fettuccine.) Set the pappardelle aside.

At the end of the turkey-marinating time, preheat the broiler. Remove the drumsticks from the casserole, pat the drumsticks dry with paper towels and lightly

dredge them in the flour. Brush the drumsticks with the oil and broil them about 3 inches below the heat source, turning them as they brown, for about 15 minutes. Set the oven temperature at 375° F. Return the drumsticks to the marinade in the casserole, then place the casserole over medium-high heat and bring the marinade to a boil. Cover the casserole tightly and put it in the oven. Braise the turkey until it is tender, turning the drumsticks from time to time so that they cook evenly — about one hour.

About 15 minutes before the end of the braising period, put the mushrooms and the pearl onions in separate saucepans over medium-high heat and cover the vegetables with water. Bring the water to a boil and cook them until they are tender — about three minutes for the mushrooms, 10 minutes for the onions. Drain both saucepans and set them aside.

Lift the drumsticks from their sauce and put them on a plate. When they are cool enough to handle, remove the skin and discard it. Shred the turkey meat with your fingers, eliminating the tendons and sinews, and set the meat aside. Remove the bundle of seasonings from the sauce and discard it. With a slotted spoon, remove the vegetables and purée them.

Skim as much fat as you can from the sauce, then combine the vegetable purée with the sauce. Stir in the turkey meat, mushrooms and pearl onions; keep the sauce warm while you cook the pasta.

Add the pappardelle to 4 quarts of boiling water with 2 teaspoons of salt. Start testing the pappardelle after one minute and cook them until they are *al dente*. Drain the pappardelle and mound them on a large heated serving dish. Pour the sauce over the pasta and serve it immediately. Pass the cheese separately.

Grated Pasta with Green Beans and Cheddar

Serves 6
Working time: about 20 minutes
Total time: about 1 hour and 20 minutes

Calories **232**
Protein **12g.**
Cholesterol **62mg.**
Total fat **6g.**
Saturated fat **4g.**
Sodium **340mg.**

1¾ cup unbleached all-purpose flour
1 egg
1 egg white
½ tsp. salt
¼ lb. green beans, stemmed, thinly sliced on the diagonal
2 cups skim milk
¼ tsp. white pepper
⅛ tsp. cayenne pepper
¾ cup grated Cheddar cheese
¼ cup fresh bread crumbs

Put the flour in a mixing bowl and form a well in the middle of the flour. Briefly beat the egg, egg white and ¼ teaspoon of the salt in another bowl, then pour the beaten egg into the flour. Mix with a large spoon until the flour begins to form clumps. Add enough cold water (1 or 2 tablespoons) to allow you to form the mixture into a ball with your hands. Work the last of the flour into the dough by hand, then turn the dough out onto a flour-dusted surface and knead it until it is firm and smooth — about five minutes. Encase the

dough in plastic wrap and place it in the freezer for at least an hour and a half to harden it.

Remove the dough, unwrap it and grate it on the coarse side of a hand grater. Blanch the green beans in boiling water for two minutes, then refresh them under cold running water. Preheat the oven to 350° F.

Bring the milk to a simmer over low heat in a large saucepan. Add the grated noodles, white pepper, cayenne pepper and the remaining ¼ teaspoon of salt. Simmer the mixture, stirring occasionally, until the noodles have absorbed almost all of the liquid — four to five minutes. Add the green beans and half of the grated cheese, and stir thoroughly.

Transfer the contents of the saucepan to an oven-proof casserole. Combine the remaining ⅜ cup of cheese with the bread crumbs and sprinkle the mixture over the top. Bake until the crust is crisp and golden — about 20 minutes — and serve hot.

Sweet-Potato Gnocchi

Serves 4
Working time: about 35 minutes
Total time: about 1 hour and 35 minutes

Calories **265**
Protein **10g.**
Cholesterol **8mg.**
Total fat **3g.**
Saturated fat **1g.**
Sodium **494mg.**

1 lb. sweet potatoes (yams), baked 1 hour at 400° F., cooled and peeled
¼ cup plain low-fat yogurt
4 tbsp. freshly grated Parmesan cheese
7 to 8 tbsp. unbleached all-purpose flour
¼ tsp. salt
¼ tsp. white pepper
¼ tsp. grated nutmeg
¼ tsp. ground cumin
3 egg whites
1 cup unsalted vegetable or chicken stock
1 oz. ham, julienned
2 tbsp. basil leaves, cut into strips

Mash the sweet potatoes in a bowl. Add the yogurt, Parmesan cheese and flour, and mix thoroughly with a fork or a wooden spoon (alternatively, put the ingredients in a blender or food processor and mix for 30 seconds, scraping the sides once). Season the mixture with the salt, pepper, nutmeg and cumin, then beat in the egg whites.

Bring to a boil 3 quarts of water containing 1½ teaspoons of salt. With two tablespoons, form the batter into football shapes, following the instructions on page 39. Drop the gnocchi directly from a spoon into the boiling water, until the pot contains six or seven. When all of the gnocchi return to the surface of the water, start timing; after three minutes, transfer the gnocchi with a slotted spoon to a lightly oiled casserole and keep them warm. Repeat this process to cook the remaining batter.

Heat the stock and pour it over the gnocchi. Scatter the ham and basil on top. Serve at once.

Shaping Sweet-Potato Gnocchi

1 *FILLING THE SPOON. Dip a tablespoon into the batter and heap a little less than a spoonful of the batter onto it. With your other hand take a second tablespoon of the same size and insert it behind the filling at a slight angle.*

2 *FORMING THE GNOCCHI. Rotate the first spoon backward and quickly scoop the batter into the second spoon with a flick of the wrist. Scoop the batter back and forth between spoons, until the gnocchi has three flattened sides.*

3 *POACHING THE GNOCCHI. After shaping the gnocchi, dip the spoon into a pot of simmering water and stir gently. The gnocchi should come free of the spoon in seconds. Shape the rest of the gnocchi the same way, cooking six or so at a time.*

Spinach Gnocchi

Serves 4
Working time: about 40 minutes
Total time: about 1 hour

Calories **265**
Protein **18g.**
Cholesterol **34mg.**
Total fat **14g.**
Saturated fat **6g.**
Sodium **500mg.**

1 medium onion, finely chopped (about 1 cup)
1 tbsp. virgin olive oil
1 oz. ham, chopped
10 oz. frozen spinach, defrosted, or 1 lb. fresh spinach, washed, stemmed, blanched in boiling water for one minute and drained
½ cup part-skim ricotta cheese
⅓ cup low-fat cottage cheese
6 tbsp. freshly grated Parmesan cheese
2 egg whites
⅛ tsp. grated nutmeg
½ cup unbleached all-purpose flour
1 tbsp. unsalted butter

In a small skillet over medium-high heat, sauté the onion in the oil until the onion is translucent — about two minutes. Add the ham and sauté for two minutes more, then transfer the contents of the skillet to a mixing bowl. Use your hands to squeeze the spinach dry. Then chop it finely and put it in the bowl with the onion and ham.

Work the ricotta and cottage cheese through a sieve into the bowl; add 4 tablespoons of the Parmesan cheese, the egg whites, nutmeg and flour. Stir the mixture well and put it into a piping bag fitted with a ½-inch plain tip. Preheat the oven to 400° F.

In a large pot, bring 4 quarts of water to a boil with 2 teaspoons of salt. Meanwhile, pipe 1-inch strips of the gnocchi mixture onto large sheets of wax paper, putting about 20 gnocchi in the center of each sheet. Pick up one of the wax-paper sheets by its edges and dip the gnocchi and paper together into the boiling water; the gnocchi will immediately separate from the paper. Discard the paper. Cook the gnocchi until they rise to the surface of the water and stay there — about two minutes. With a slotted spoon, transfer them to a baking dish. Cook the remaining batches of gnocchi the same way.

Dust the gnocchi with the remaining 2 tablespoons of Parmesan cheese and dot them with the butter. Bake the gnocchi until they are sizzling — about 20 minutes — and serve them immediately.

Curry Fettuccine with Chicken and Avocado

Serves 6
Working time: about 45 minutes
Total time: about 2 hours and 15 minutes

Calories **360**
Protein **25g.**
Cholesterol **96mg.**
Total fat **14g.**
Saturated fat **2g.**
Sodium **482mg.**

basic pasta dough (recipe, page 15), with 1½ tsp. curry powder added to the flour
1 cup plain low-fat yogurt
¾ tsp. curry powder
¾ tsp. salt
1 garlic clove, crushed
5 tbsp. fresh lemon juice
4 chicken breast halves, skinned and boned (about 1 lb.)
½ avocado, peeled and cut into ½-inch cubes (about ½ cup)
¾ lb. carrots, peeled and sliced into ½-inch-thick rounds
freshly ground black pepper
2 tbsp. safflower oil
2 tbsp. finely chopped fresh parsley, preferably Italian

In a large, shallow bowl, combine ½ cup of the yogurt, ½ teaspoon of the curry powder, ¼ teaspoon of the salt, the garlic and 3 tablespoons of the lemon juice. Arrange the chicken pieces in the bowl in a single layer and spoon the yogurt mixture over them. Let the chicken marinate in the refrigerator for at least two hours, turning it every 30 minutes.

Put the avocado cubes in a small bowl. Pour the remaining 2 tablespoons of lemon juice over them, then toss the cubes gently to coat them. Set aside.

Roll out the pasta dough and cut it into fettuccine (*technique, pages 12-13*). Set the fettuccine aside.

Put the carrots and the remaining ½ teaspoon of salt in a saucepan. Pour in just enough water to cover the carrots, then bring the water to a boil. Reduce the heat to low, cover the pan, and simmer the carrots until they are tender — 15 to 20 minutes. Drain the carrots, reserving ¼ cup of their cooking liquid.

In a food mill or food processor, purée the carrots with their reserved cooking liquid. Add the remaining ½ cup of yogurt and the remaining ¼ teaspoon of curry powder, and purée again. Transfer the mixture to a small saucepan and warm it over low heat. Do not let the sauce boil or the yogurt will separate.

Meanwhile, wipe the marinade from the chicken breast halves and discard it. Sprinkle the chicken with some pepper. Heat the oil in a heavy-bottomed skillet over medium-high heat. Add the chicken breasts to the skillet and sauté them until they are cooked through — four to five minutes on each side. Cut the meat into chunks; cover the chunks and set them aside in a warm place.

Add the fettuccine to 3 quarts of boiling water with 1½ teaspoons of salt. Start testing the fettuccine after one minute and cook it until it is *al dente*.

To assemble the dish, ladle enough of the carrot purée into a heated serving dish to cover the bottom. Arrange the fettuccine on top of the purée. Spoon the remaining purée in a ring around the center, then mound the chicken in the center. Scatter the avocado cubes and parsley over the chicken, and serve the dish immediately.

2

One of the earliest (and best) of convenience foods, dried pasta fills glass storage jars in a kitchen reminiscent of pasta's Mediterranean homeland.

The Most Varied of Foods

Dried pasta speaks Italian. Any list of available types is almost operatic in the musical sound of its Italian names — from the familiar spaghetti, linguine and lasagne to the more exotic radiatori, perciatelli and fusilli. With well over a hundred shapes to tempt the cook and numberless sauces to accompany them, dried pasta ranks among the most varied of foods.

In pasta, as so often in architecture, form can follow function. All those shapes are not just intended to please the eye; many have good reason for their existence. Understanding why they look the way they do can make you a better pasta cook. Consider the spaghetti family. In addition to the familiar pasta most of us have always eaten, it includes capellini (angel hair) and vermicelli; among its many cousins are linguine and fettuccine. Although they all share a common trait — their ruler-straight lengths — they are not all to be sauced alike. The delicate capellini and vermicelli cry out for light treatment — perhaps something as simple as fresh chopped tomatoes, herbs and a little olive oil. The sturdier linguine and fettuccine will hold their own against a thick, strongly flavored sauce.

Tubular pastas demand a sauce that will cling to them inside and out. Shells and dimpled shapes are exactly right for holding puddles of sauce and bits of meat or fish. Twists allow a luscious sauce to wrap itself around them, yet they will also accept a light vinaigrette when served cold as a salad.

Sauce's variety is limited only by the cook's imagination. This section alone includes 53 different kinds, all of them original — from one made with Stilton cheese and Port to others of collard greens and lobster, and mushrooms, yogurt and poppy seeds. At the same time it offers such audacious combinations as these, the section takes some fresh approaches to familiar dishes. There is, for example, lasagne prepared with Gorgonzola cheese and escarole. Pasta with basil pesto is the inspiration for an arugula pesto, greener than its prototype yet every bit as flavorsome. Another dish starts with the fresh ingredients of a basil pesto and instead of reducing them to a thick purée adds them directly to the pasta. The section even includes a couple of pasta dishes cooked right in the sauce. The pasta's starch thickens the sauce, while the sauce flavors the pasta. What could be easier?

A Pasta Primer

LONG THIN

SHORT TUBULAR

ditalini
salad macaroni

elbows

ziti

penne
mostaccioli

penne rigati
mostaccioli rigati

rigatoni

perciatelli
bucatini

spaghetti

thin spaghetti
spaghettini

vermicelli

capellini

fusilli

manicotti

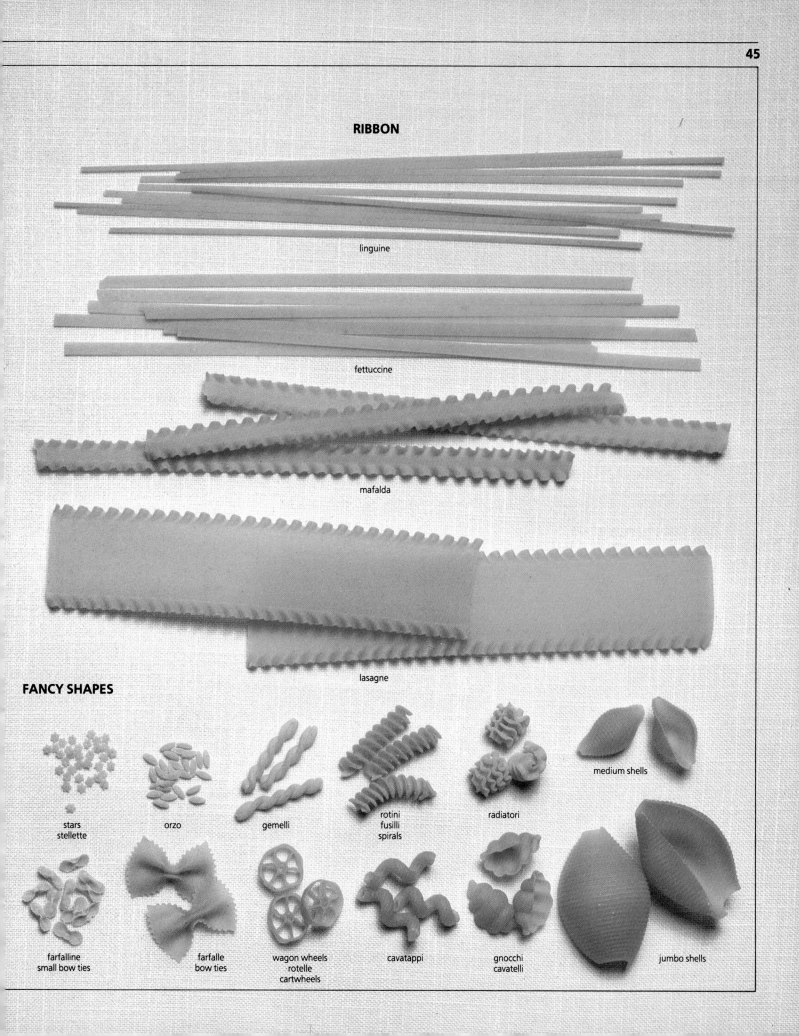

RIBBON

linguine

fettuccine

mafalda

lasagne

FANCY SHAPES

stars
stellette

orzo

gemelli

rotini
fusilli
spirals

radiatori

medium shells

farfalline
small bow ties

farfalle
bow ties

wagon wheels
rotelle
cartwheels

cavatappi

gnocchi
cavatelli

jumbo shells

Linguine with Limas and Grainy Mustard

Serves 4
Working (and total) time: about 20 minutes

Calories **346**
Protein **12g.**
Cholesterol **16mg.**
Total fat **8g.**
Saturated fat **4g.**
Sodium **324mg.**

8 oz. linguine
3 ripe plum tomatoes (about ½ lb.)
¾ cup unsalted chicken stock
1 cup frozen baby lima beans
¼ tsp. salt
2 scallions, trimmed and thinly sliced
1½ tbsp. grainy mustard
2 tbsp. unsalted butter

Place a tomato on a cutting surface with its stem end down. With a small, sharp knife, cut wide strips of flesh from the tomato, discarding its seeds and juice. Slice each piece of tomato flesh into ¼-inch-wide strips and set them aside. Repeat the process with the remaining tomatoes.

Pour the stock into a large, heavy-bottomed skillet over medium heat and bring it to a simmer. Add the lima beans and salt, and cook for six minutes. Stir in the scallions and mustard; simmer for one minute more. Add the butter and the tomato strips, then simmer the mixture for an additional two minutes, stirring once.

Meanwhile, cook the linguine in 3 quarts of boiling water with 1½ teaspoons of salt. Start testing the pasta after 10 minutes and cook it until it is *al dente*. Drain the linguine and transfer it to the skillet with the lima bean mixture. Toss well and serve immediately.

EDITOR'S NOTE: *If plum tomatoes are not available, an equivalent amount of another variety of red tomato may be used.*

Penne Rigati with Mushrooms and Tarragon

Serves 4
Working (and total) time: about 45 minutes

Calories **384**
Protein **11g.**
Cholesterol **0mg.**
Total fat **8g.**
Saturated fat **1g.**
Sodium **387mg.**

8 oz. penne rigati (or other short, tubular pasta)
½ oz. dried porcini mushrooms (cepes) (about 2 tbsp.)
2 tbsp. virgin olive oil
1 small onion, finely chopped
½ lb. button mushrooms, cut into ¼-inch dice
½ tsp. salt
freshly ground black pepper
3 garlic cloves, finely chopped
1 cup dry white wine
1½ lb. tomatoes, peeled, seeded and chopped (about 2 cups)
⅓ cup chopped fresh parsley
2 tbsp. chopped fresh tarragon

Pour 1 cup of hot water over the dried porcini mushrooms and soak them until they are soft — about 20 minutes. Drain the porcini and reserve their soaking liquid. Cut the drained porcini into ¼-inch pieces.

Heat the oil in a large, heavy-bottomed skillet over medium heat. Add the onion and sauté it until it turns translucent — about four minutes. Add the porcini and button mushrooms, salt and pepper. Cook until the mushrooms begin to brown — about five minutes. Add the garlic and the wine, and cook the mixture until the liquid is reduced to approximately 2 tablespoons — about five minutes more.

Add the penne rigati to 3 quarts of boiling water with 1½ teaspoons of salt. Start testing the pasta after 10 minutes and continue to cook it until it is *al dente*.

While the penne rigati is cooking, pour the reserved porcini-soaking liquid into the skillet containing the mushrooms and cook until the liquid is reduced to approximately ¼ cup — about five minutes. Stir in the tomatoes and cook the mixture until it is heated through — about three minutes more. Drain the pasta and add it to the skillet along with the chopped parsley and tarragon. Toss well and serve.

Perciatelli with Carrot and Zucchini Serpents

Serves 6 as an appetizer
Working time: about 20 minutes
Total time: about 30 minutes

Calories **210**
Protein **6g.**
Cholesterol **2mg.**
Total fat **5g.**
Saturated fat **1g.**
Sodium **72mg.**

8 oz. perciatelli or linguine
2 carrots
3 medium zucchini, washed, ends removed
2 tbsp. virgin olive oil
6 large garlic cloves, peeled, each sliced into 4 or 5 pieces
2 anchovy fillets, finely chopped
¾ cup thinly sliced red onion
freshly ground black pepper

Fashion the carrot and zucchini serpents: Pressing down hard on a sharp vegetable peeler, grate along the length of a carrot to detach a wide strip. Continue removing strips until you reach the woody core, then turn the carrot over and repeat the process on the other side. Peel strips from the other carrot in the same manner, then cut each strip lengthwise into ¼-inch-wide serpents. With a small, sharp knife, cut a long strip about 1 inch wide and ¼ inch thick from the outside of a zucchini. Continue cutting strips to remove the green outer portion of all the zucchini. Discard the seedy inner cores. Cut each strip lengthwise into serpents ⅛ inch wide.

Put 3 quarts of water on to boil with 1½ teaspoons of salt. Heat the oil in a large, heavy-bottomed skillet over low heat. Add the garlic slices and cook them, stirring occasionally, until they are golden brown on both sides — 10 to 15 minutes.

About five minutes after adding the garlic to the pan, drop the pasta into the boiling water. Start testing the pasta after 12 minutes and continue to cook it until it is al dente.

When the garlic slices have turned golden brown, add the anchovy fillets, onion, carrots and zucchini to the skillet; cover the skillet, and cook for three minutes. Remove the cover and cook the mixture, stirring frequently, for three minutes more.

Drain the pasta and immediately add it to the skillet. Add some pepper, toss well, and serve at once.

Fettuccine with Artichokes and Tomatoes

Serves 4
Working time: about 25 minutes
Total time: about 50 minutes

Calories **289**
Protein **12g.**
Cholesterol **7mg.**
Total fat **3g.**
Saturated fat **1g.**
Sodium **345mg.**

8 oz. fettuccine (or other narrow ribbon pasta)
1½ lb. ripe tomatoes, peeled and chopped, seeds and juice reserved, or 28 oz. unsalted canned whole tomatoes, drained and chopped
1 onion, chopped
1 carrot, peeled, quartered lengthwise and cut into ¼-inch pieces
1 tsp. fresh thyme, or ¼ tsp. dried thyme leaves
1 tsp. chopped fresh rosemary, or ¼ tsp. dried rosemary
¼ tsp. salt
freshly ground black pepper
3 fresh artichoke bottoms, rubbed with the juice of 1 lemon
1 tbsp. red wine vinegar or cider vinegar
¼ cup freshly grated Romano or Parmesan cheese

Put the chopped tomatoes, onion, carrot, the thyme and rosemary if you are using fresh herbs, and the salt and pepper in a saucepan over medium-high heat. Bring the mixture to a boil, reduce the heat to low, and simmer the mixture for five minutes.

Slice the artichoke bottoms into strips ⅛ inch wide and add them to the pan. If you are using dried herbs, add them now. Pour in the vinegar and simmer the mixture, uncovered, for 15 minutes. Add the reserved tomato seeds and juice, if you are using fresh tomatoes, and continue cooking until most of the liquid has evaporated and the artichoke bottoms are tender but not mushy — about 15 minutes more.

Approximately 15 minutes before the vegetables finish cooking, add the fettuccine to 3 quarts boiling water with 1½ teaspoons of salt. Start testing the pasta after 10 minutes and cook it until it is *al dente*. Drain the fettuccine and add it immediately to the sauce. Sprinkle the cheese over the top, toss lightly and serve.

Sweet-and-Sour Cabbage Manicotti

Serves 6
Working time: about 45 minutes
Total time: about 1 hour and 30 minutes

Calories **293**
Protein **9g.**
Cholesterol **11mg.**
Total fat **6g.**
Saturated fat **3g.**
Sodium **192mg.**

12 manicotti tubes (about 8 oz.)
2 tbsp. unsalted butter
1 small onion, finely chopped
1 lb. green cabbage, shredded
1 carrot, peeled and grated
1 apple, peeled, cored and grated
¼ tsp. salt
7 or 8 ripe tomatoes (about 2½ lb.), quartered
1 tbsp. dark brown sugar
2 tbsp. white wine vinegar
¼ cup raisins
1 cup unsalted chicken stock

To prepare the cabbage stuffing, melt the butter in a large, heavy-bottomed skillet over medium heat.

Add the onion and sauté it until it turns translucent — about four minutes. Pour enough water into the skillet to fill it ¼ inch deep. Stir in the cabbage, carrot, apple and ⅛ teaspoon of the salt. Cover the skillet and steam the vegetables and apple, adding more water as necessary, until they are soft — about 30 minutes. Set the skillet aside.

Meanwhile, pour ¼ cup of water into a saucepan over medium-high heat. Add the tomatoes and cook them, stirring frequently, until they are quite soft — about 20 minutes. Transfer the tomatoes to a sieve or food mill and allow their clear liquid to drain off. Discard the liquid and purée the tomatoes into a bowl. Stir in the brown sugar, vinegar, raisins and the remaining ⅛ teaspoon of salt.

To prepare the manicotti, add the tubes to 4 quarts of boiling water with 2 teaspoons of salt. Start testing the manicotti after 15 minutes and cook them until they are *al dente*. With a slotted spoon, transfer the tubes to a large bowl of cold water.

Preheat the oven to 400° F. Thoroughly drain the manicotti tubes and fill each one carefully with about ⅔ cup of the cabbage stuffing. Arrange the tubes in a

single layer in a large baking dish. Pour the stock over the tubes and cover the dish tightly with aluminum foil. Bake for 30 minutes. Ten minutes before serving time, transfer the sauce from the bowl to a saucepan and bring it to a boil. Reduce the heat to low and let the sauce simmer gently while the manicotti finish cooking. Serve the manicotti immediately; pass the sauce separately.

EDITOR'S NOTE: *To allow for manicotti tubes that may tear during cooking or while being stuffed, add one or two extra tubes to the boiling water. The manicotti may be assembled in advance and refrigerated for up to 24 hours before the stock is added and the dish is baked.*

Penne with Squid in Tomato-Fennel Sauce

Serves 4
Working time: about 35 minutes
Total time: about 1 hour

Calories **361**
Protein **20g.**
Cholesterol **119mg.**
Total fat **5g.**
Saturated fat **1g.**
Sodium **314mg.**

8 oz. penne (or other short, tubular pasta)
4 medium squid (about ¾ lb.)
1 tbsp. safflower oil
¼ cup anise-flavored liqueur, or 1 tsp. fennel seeds
1½ lb. tomatoes, peeled, seeded and chopped, or 14 oz. unsalted canned tomatoes, drained and chopped
1 head fennel, stalks discarded and the bulb grated
6 scallions, trimmed and finely chopped
¼ tsp. salt
freshly ground black pepper

To clean a squid, first gently pull the quill-shaped pen out of its body pouch. Then, holding the body pouch in one hand and the head in the other, pull the two sections apart; the viscera will come away with the head. Rinse the body pouch thoroughly and rub off the thin, purplish skin covering it. Remove the triangular fins and skin them too, then slice them into strips. Cut the tentacles from the head, slicing just below the eyes. Cut out the hard beak from the center of the tentacles and discard it. Slice the body pouch into thin rings. Repeat these steps to clean the other three squid.

Heat the oil in a large, heavy-bottomed skillet over medium-high heat. Sauté the squid in the oil for one to two minutes. Pour in the liqueur if you are using it, and cook the mixture for 30 seconds more. With a slotted spoon, transfer the squid to a plate. Add the tomato, fennel, the fennel seeds if you are using them, and the scallions to the skillet. Reduce the heat to low and simmer the mixture, stirring occasionally, until the fennel is soft — 20 to 25 minutes.

When the fennel has been simmering for about 10 minutes, add the penne to 3 quarts of boiling water with 1½ teaspoons of salt. Start testing the pasta after 10 minutes and cook it until it is *al dente*.

When the pasta is almost done, return the squid to the sauce and gently heat it through — two to three minutes. Season the sauce with the salt and the pepper. Drain the pasta, transfer it to a bowl and toss it with the sauce. Serve immediately.

Spaghetti with Fresh Basil, Pine Nuts and Cheese

Serves 4
Working (and total) time: about 15 minutes

Calories **362**
Protein **14g.**
Cholesterol **15mg.**
Total fat **13g.**
Saturated fat **3g.**
Sodium **414mg.**

8 oz. spaghetti
1 tbsp. virgin olive oil
1 garlic clove, crushed
1 cup shredded basil leaves, plus several whole leaves reserved for garnish
½ cup unsalted chicken stock
¼ cup pine nuts (about 1 oz.), toasted in a small, dry skillet over medium heat
½ cup freshly grated Romano cheese
¼ tsp. salt
freshly ground black pepper

To prepare the sauce, first pour the oil into a skillet set over medium heat. When the oil is hot, add the garlic and cook it, stirring constantly, for about 30 seconds. Reduce the heat to low. Stir in the shredded basil leaves and allow them to wilt — approximately 30 seconds. Pour in the stock and simmer the liquid gently while you cook the pasta.

Add the spaghetti to 3 quarts of boiling water with 1½ teaspoons of salt. Start testing the pasta after 10 minutes and cook it until it is *al dente.*

Drain the pasta and add it to the skillet with the basil. Toss well to coat the pasta. Add the pine nuts, cheese, salt and some pepper, and toss again. Serve at once, garnished with the whole basil leaves.

Gorgonzola Lasagne

Serves 8
Working time: about 45 minutes
Total time: about 1 hour and 30 minutes

Calories **207**
Protein **9g.**
Cholesterol **13mg.**
Total fat **8g.**
Saturated fat **3g.**
Sodium **244mg.**

8 oz. lasagne
4 red peppers
2 red onions (about ¾ lb.), sliced into ½-inch-thick rounds
2 tbsp. fresh lemon juice
3 tsp. fresh thyme, or ¾ tsp. dried thyme leaves
2 tbsp. virgin olive oil
1 small head escarole (about 1 lb.), washed, trimmed and sliced crosswise into 1-inch-wide strips
½ tsp. salt
freshly ground black pepper
¼ cup freshly grated Parmesan cheese
4 oz. Gorgonzola cheese, broken into small pieces

Preheat the broiler. Arrange the peppers in the center of a baking sheet with the onion slices surrounding them. Broil the vegetables until the peppers are blis-tered on all sides and the onions are lightly browned — 10 to 15 minutes. (You will need to turn the peppers a few times, the onions once.) Put the peppers in a bowl, cover it with plastic wrap, and set it aside. Separate the onion slices into rings and reserve them as well.

Cook the lasagne in 3 quarts of boiling unsalted water with the lemon juice for seven minutes — the pasta will be slightly underdone. Drain the pasta and run cold water over it.

Peel the peppers when they are cool enough to han-dle, working over a bowl to catch the juices. Remove the stem, seeds and ribs from each pepper. Set one pepper aside and slice the remaining three into length-wise strips about ¾ inch wide. Strain the pepper juices and reserve them.

Quarter the reserved whole pepper; purée the pieces in a food processor or blender with the pepper juices and 2 teaspoons of the fresh thyme or ½ tea-spoon of the dried thyme. Preheat the oven to 350° F.

Heat the oil in a large, heavy-bottomed skillet over medium-high heat. Add the escarole, ¼ teaspoon of the salt, the remaining teaspoon of fresh thyme or ¼ ▶

teaspoon of dried thyme, and a generous grinding of black pepper. Sauté the escarole until it is wilted and almost all the liquid has evaporated — about five minutes. Remove the pan from the heat.

Line the bottom of a baking dish with a layer of the lasagne. Cover this layer with half of the escarole and sprinkle it with 1 tablespoon of the Parmesan cheese. Spread half of the pepper strips over the top, then cover them with half of the onion rings. Build a second layer of lasagne, escarole, Parmesan cheese, pepper strips and onion rings, this time topping the onion rings with half of the pepper purée. Cover the second level with a final layer of lasagne, and spread the remaining purée over the top. Scatter the Gorgonzola cheese evenly over the pepper sauce and sprinkle the remaining 2 tablespoons of Parmesan cheese over all.

Bake the lasagne for 30 minutes. Let the dish stand for 10 minutes to allow the flavors to meld.

Pasta Salad with Lobster and Snow Peas

THE RADIATORI CALLED FOR HERE IS A PASTA WITH RIDGES THAT RESEMBLE THE HEATING COILS OF A RADIATOR. COOKING THE RADIATORI IN THE LOBSTER WATER INFUSES THE PASTA WITH THE FLAVOR OF THE SHELLFISH.

Serves 4
Working time: about 40 minutes
Total time: about 1 hour

Calories **375**
Protein **17g.**
Cholesterol **41mg.**
Total fat **12g.**
Saturated fat **1g.**
Sodium **271mg.**

8 oz. radiatori (or other fancy pasta)
¼ cup very thinly sliced shallots
1 tbsp. red wine vinegar
3 tbsp. virgin olive oil
2 garlic cloves, lightly crushed
¼ tsp. salt
freshly ground black pepper
1 live lobster (about 1½ lb.)
2 tbsp. lemon juice
½ lb. snow peas, stems and strings removed, sliced in half with a diagonal cut
1 tbsp. chopped fresh basil or Italian parsley

Pour enough water into a large pot to fill it about 1 inch deep. Bring the water to a boil and add the lobster. Cover the pot tightly and steam the lobster until it turns a bright reddish orange — about 12 minutes.

In the meantime, put half of the shallots in a bowl with the vinegar and let them stand for five minutes. Whisk in 2 tablespoons of the oil, then stir in the garlic, ⅛ teaspoon of the salt, and some pepper. Set the vinaigrette aside.

Remove the lobster from the pot and set it on a dish to catch the juices. Pour 2 quarts of water into the pot along with 1 tablespoon of the lemon juice, and bring the liquid to a boil.

When the lobster has cooled enough to handle, twist off the tail and claws from the body. Crack the shell and remove the meat from the tail and claws. Add the shells and the body to the boiling liquid and cook for 10 minutes. Cut the meat into ½-inch pieces and set it aside in a bowl.

Use a slotted spoon to remove the shells from the boiling liquid; then add the pasta. Start testing after 13 minutes and cook the pasta until it is *al dente*.

While the pasta is cooking, pour the remaining tablespoon of oil into a large, heavy-bottomed skillet over medium high heat. Add the snow peas along with the remaining 2 tablespoons of shallots and ⅛ teaspoon of salt. Cook, stirring constantly, until the snow peas turn bright green — about one and a half minutes. Scrape the contents of the skillet into the bowl with the lobster.

When the pasta finishes cooking, drain it and rinse it briefly under cold water. Remove and discard the garlic from the vinaigrette, then combine the vinaigrette with the pasta. Add the lobster mixture, the basil, the remaining tablespoon of lemon juice and some more pepper, and toss well.

EDITOR'S NOTE: *Although the pasta salad may be served immediately, allowing it to stand for 30 minutes will meld its flavors. Alternatively, the salad may be served chilled.*

Pinto Beans
and Wagon Wheels

PINTO BEANS CONTAIN TOXINS CALLED LECTINS. TO DESTROY
THE LECTINS, BE SURE TO BOIL THE BEANS FOR 10 MINUTES BEFORE
ADDING THEM TO THE DISH.

Serves 4
Working time: about 25 minutes
Total time: about 9 hours and 30 minutes

Calories **575**
Protein **32g.**
Cholesterol **37mg.**
Total fat **13g.**
Saturated fat **3g.**
Sodium **471mg.**

8 oz. wagon wheels (or other fancy-shaped or short, tubular pasta)
1 cup pinto beans, soaked for eight hours in 3 cups water and drained
2 tbsp. safflower oil
6 oz. boneless top round of beef, cut into ½-inch cubes
1 small onion, finely chopped
1 green pepper, seeded, deribbed and cut into ½-inch squares
1 garlic clove, very finely chopped
2½ lb. ripe tomatoes, peeled, seeded and chopped, or 28 oz. unsalted canned whole tomatoes, drained and chopped
5 drops hot red-pepper sauce
1 tbsp. cilantro, coarsely chopped
freshly ground black pepper
½ tsp. salt
¼ cup grated Cheddar cheese

Cook the beans in 3 cups of boiling water for 10 minutes, then drain them and set them aside.

While the beans are boiling, heat the safflower oil in a large, heavy-bottomed skillet over medium-high heat. Brown the beef in the oil, stirring frequently, for three minutes. Remove the meat from the skillet with a slotted spoon and set it aside.

Cook the onion and green pepper in the oil remaining in the skillet until the onion turns translucent — about three minutes. Add the garlic and cook for half a minute more, then return the beef to the skillet. Stir in the tomatoes, pinto beans and 1 cup of warm water, and bring the mixture to a simmer. Cover the skillet and reduce the heat to low. Simmer the mixture until the beans are tender — about 1 hour and 10 minutes.

Approximately 10 minutes before the beans finish cooking, add the wagon wheels to 3 quarts of boiling

water with 1½ teaspoons of salt. Start testing the wheels after eight minutes and continue to cook them until they are *al dente*.

Drain the wagon wheels and add them to the bean mixture; stir in the red-pepper sauce, cilantro, black pepper and salt. Simmer for three minutes more, then transfer the contents of the skillet to a serving dish;

sprinkle the cheese over the top and serve at once.

EDITOR'S NOTE: *As a time-saving alternative to soaking the pinto beans for eight hours, boil them in 3 cups of water for two minutes, then remove the pot from the heat, cover it, and let the beans soak for one hour. Drain the beans and boil them in fresh water for 10 minutes, as above, before adding them to the skillet.*

Gnocchi with Spicy Carrot Sauce

Serves 6 as an appetizer or side dish
Working time: about 15 minutes
Total time: about 1 hour

Calories **187**
Protein **7g.**
Cholesterol **39mg.**
Total fat **4g.**
Saturated fat **2g.**
Sodium **199mg.**

8 oz. dried gnocchi (or other fancy-shaped pasta)
½ lb. carrots, peeled and finely chopped (about 1½ cups)
1 celery stalk, finely chopped
4 garlic cloves, finely chopped
¼ tsp. crushed red pepper
1 tbsp. fresh thyme, or 1 tsp. dried thyme leaves
2 cups unsalted chicken or vegetable stock
¼ cup red wine vinegar
1 tbsp. unsalted butter
¼ tsp. salt
freshly ground black pepper

Put the carrots, celery, garlic, red pepper, thyme and enough water to cover them in a large skillet. Bring the mixture to a boil, then cover the pan and reduce the heat to medium. Simmer the vegetables until they are tender — about 20 minutes.

Pour 1 cup of the stock into the carrot mixture and cook until the liquid is reduced to approximately ¼ cup — about 10 minutes. Add the remaining cup of stock and the vinegar, and cook until only ¼ cup of liquid remains — about 10 minutes more.

While you are reducing the second cup of stock, cook the pasta in 3 quarts of boiling water with 1½ teaspoons of salt. Start testing the pasta after five minutes and cook it until it is *al dente*.

Stir the butter, salt and pepper into the sauce. Drain the pasta, put it in a bowl, and toss it with the sauce.

Chilled Rotini
with Arugula Pesto

Serves 4
Working time: about 25 minutes
Total time: about 2 hours

Calories **536**
Protein **17g.**
Cholesterol **8mg.**
Total fat **22g.**
Saturated fat **4g.**
Sodium **397mg.**

12 oz. rotini
2 cups arugula, washed, cleaned and stemmed
1 small garlic clove, coarsely chopped
¼ cup pine nuts
3 tbsp. virgin olive oil
1 tbsp. safflower oil
½ cup freshly grated Parmesan cheese
¼ tsp. salt
freshly ground black pepper

1 red pepper, seeded, deribbed and finely diced
2 tbsp. balsamic vinegar, or 1 tbsp. red wine vinegar

Add the rotini to 4 quarts of boiling water with 2 teaspoons of salt. Start testing the pasta after eight minutes and cook it until it is *al dente*.

Meanwhile, prepare the pesto: Put the arugula, garlic, pine nuts, olive oil and safflower oil in a blender or food processor. Blend for two minutes, stopping two or three times to scrape down the sides. Add the cheese and the ¼ teaspoon of salt; blend the mixture briefly to form a purée.

Drain the pasta, transfer it to a large bowl, and season it with some black pepper. Add the diced red pepper, the vinegar and pesto, and toss well. Chill the pasta salad in the refrigerator for an hour or two before serving it.

Ziti with Italian Sausage and Red Peppers

Serves 4
Working time: about 30 minutes
Total time: about 40 minutes

Calories **298**
Protein **11g.**
Cholesterol **12mg.**
Total fat **7g.**
Saturated fat **2g.**
Sodium **332mg.**

8 oz. ziti (or other fancy tubular pasta)
3 red peppers
2 spicy Italian sausage links (about 4 oz.)
2 garlic cloves, finely chopped
2 tsp. fresh thyme, or ½ tsp. dried thyme leaves
1 large tomato, peeled, seeded and puréed
1 tbsp. red wine vinegar
⅛ tsp. salt

Preheat the broiler. Broil the peppers about two inches below the heat source, turning them from time to time, until they are blackened all over — 15 to 18 minutes. Put the peppers in a bowl and cover it with plastic wrap. The trapped steam will loosen their skins.

Squeeze the sausages out of their casings and break the meat into small pieces; sauté the pieces over medium-high heat until they are browned — about three minutes. Remove the pan from the heat and stir in the garlic and the thyme.

Add the pasta to 3 quarts of boiling water with 1½ teaspoons of salt; start testing it after 10 minutes and cook it until it is *al dente*.

While the pasta is cooking, peel the peppers, working over a bowl to catch the juices. Remove and discard the stems, seeds and ribs from the peppers; strain the juices and reserve them. Slice the peppers lengthwise into thin strips.

Set the skillet containing the sausage mixture over medium heat. Add the pepper strips and their reserved juices, the puréed tomato, the vinegar and the ⅛ teaspoon of salt. Simmer the sauce until it thickens and is reduced by about one third — five to seven minutes.

Drain the pasta, return it to the pot, and combine it with the sauce. Cover the pot and let the pasta stand for five minutes to allow the flavors to blend.

Vermicelli, Onions and Peas

Serves 8 as a side dish
Working time: about 15 minutes
Total time: about 1 hour

Calories **186**		½ lb. vermicelli or spaghettini
Protein **5g.**		2 tbsp. virgin olive oil
Cholesterol **0mg.**		4 cups chopped onion
Total fat **4g.**		1 leek, trimmed, cleaned and thinly sliced
Saturated fat **1g.**		¼ tsp. salt
Sodium **122mg.**		freshly ground black pepper
		1 cup dry white wine
		½ cup peas

Heat the oil in a large, heavy-bottomed skillet over low heat. Add the onion, leek, salt and a generous grinding of pepper. Cover the skillet tightly and cook, stirring frequently to keep the onions from sticking, until the vegetables are very soft — about 45 minutes.

Cook the pasta in 3 quarts of boiling water with 1½ teaspoons of salt. Start testing the pasta after seven minutes and cook it until it is *al dente*.

While the pasta is cooking, finish the sauce: Pour the wine into the skillet and raise the heat to high. Cook

the mixture until the liquid is reduced to about ¼ cup — approximately five minutes. Stir in the peas, cover the pan, and cook for another minute or two to heat the peas through. If you are using fresh peas, increase the cooking time to five minutes.

Drain the pasta and transfer it to a serving dish; pour the contents of the skillet over the top and toss well. Serve immediately.

Lasagne Roll-Ups

Serves 6
Working time: about 45 minutes
Total time: about 1 hour and 10 minutes

Calories **446**
Protein **24g.**
Cholesterol **35mg.**
Total fat **16g.**
Saturated fat **7g.**
Sodium **342mg.**

12 lasagne
1 lb. part-skim ricotta cheese
4 oz. part-skim mozzarella, shredded
2 small broccoli stalks, steamed for 5 minutes, drained and chopped (about 2 cups)
1 cup sliced fresh mushrooms
2 scallions, trimmed and chopped
2 tbsp. chopped fresh basil, or 2 tsp. dried basil
1 tbsp. chopped fresh oregano, or 1 tsp. dried oregano
¼ cup chopped fresh parsley
Tomato sauce
2 tbsp. safflower oil
1 onion, coarsely chopped
2 small carrots, peeled and coarsely chopped
2 celery stalks, trimmed and coarsely chopped
2 garlic cloves, thinly sliced
3 tbsp. chopped fresh basil, or 1 tbsp. dried basil
freshly ground black pepper
1 bay leaf
⅔ cup Madeira
2½ lb. ripe tomatoes, peeled, seeded and chopped, or 28 oz. unsalted canned whole tomatoes, drained and chopped
2 tbsp. tomato paste
½ cup unsweetened applesauce
3 tbsp. freshly grated Parmesan cheese

To make the sauce, pour the oil into a large, heavy-bottomed saucepan over medium-high heat. Add the onion, carrot and celery. Sauté the mixture, stirring frequently, for two minutes. Add the garlic and cook for one minute more. Stir in the basil, pepper, bay leaf and Madeira. Bring the liquid to a boil and cook it until it is reduced by about half — two to three minutes. Add the tomatoes, tomato paste and applesauce. As soon as the liquid returns to a boil, reduce the heat to low and gently simmer the sauce for 30 to 35 minutes. Remove the bay leaf and transfer the sauce to a food processor or blender. Purée the sauce and return it to the saucepan. Stir in the grated Parmesan cheese and set the pan aside.

Preheat the oven to 350° F. Add the lasagne to 4 quarts of boiling water with 2 teaspoons of salt. Start testing the pasta after 12 minutes and cook it until it is *al dente.* Drain the pieces and spread them on a clean dish towel to dry.

In a large bowl, mix the ricotta, mozzarella, broccoli, mushrooms, scallions, basil, oregano and parsley.

To assemble the dish, spread 1 cup of the tomato sauce over the bottom of an 11-by-13-inch baking pan. Spread about ¼ cup of the cheese-and-vegetable mixture over a lasagne strip; starting at one end, roll up the strip. Place the roll, seam side down, in the baking pan. Repeat the process with the remaining lasagne strips and filling. Pour the rest of the sauce over the rolls and cover the pan tightly with aluminum foil. Bake the rolls for 20 minutes, then remove the foil and bake them for 15 to 20 minutes more. Serve the lasagne roll-ups piping hot from the pan.

EDITOR'S NOTE: *To compensate for lasagne that may tear during cooking, add one or two extra strips to the boiling water.*

Vermicelli Salad with Sliced Pork

Serves 6
Working (and total) time: about 30 minutes

Calories **206**
Protein **9g.**
Cholesterol **14mg.**
Total fat **3g.**
Saturated fat **1g.**
Sodium **235mg.**

8 oz. vermicelli (or other long, thin pasta)
½ tbsp. safflower oil
4 oz. pork loin, fat trimmed, meat pounded flat and sliced into thin strips
2 garlic cloves, finely chopped
3 carrots, peeled and julienned (about 2 cups)
4 celery stalks, trimmed and julienned (about 2 cups)
2 tsp. dark sesame oil
¼ tsp. salt
freshly ground black pepper
6 drops hot red-pepper sauce
2 tbsp. rice vinegar
1 tsp. cream sherry

Break the vermicelli into thirds and drop it into 3 quarts of boiling water with 1½ teaspoons of salt. Start testing the pasta after five minutes and continue to cook it until it is *al dente*.

While the pasta is cooking, heat the safflower oil in a wok or a large skillet over medium-high heat. Stir fry the pork strips in the oil for two minutes. Add the garlic and cook for 30 seconds, stirring constantly to keep it from burning. Add the carrot and celery, and stir fry the mixture for two minutes more.

Drain the pasta and toss it in a large bowl with the pork-and-vegetable mixture. Drizzle the sesame oil over the pasta, then sprinkle it with the ¼ teaspoon of salt, the black pepper and the hot-pepper sauce, and toss thoroughly. Pour the vinegar and sherry over the salad and toss it once more. Serve the salad at room temperature or chilled.

Penne with Canadian Bacon and Mushroom Sauce

Serves 8
Working time: about 15 minutes
Total time: about 45 minutes

Calories **317**
Protein **11g.**
Cholesterol **7mg.**
Total fat **6g.**
Saturated fat **2g.**
Sodium **214mg.**

1 lb. penne (or other short, tubular pasta)
2½ lb. Italian plum tomatoes, quartered, or 28 oz. unsalted canned whole tomatoes, drained
4 whole dried red chili peppers
2 tbsp. virgin olive oil
1 onion, finely chopped
1 lb. mushrooms, wiped clean and sliced
2 oz. Canadian bacon, julienned
4 garlic cloves, finely chopped
½ cup dry white wine
2 tbsp. chopped fresh parsley, preferably Italian
1 tbsp. unsalted butter

In a large saucepan, combine the tomatoes, chili peppers and ¼ cup of water. Cook over medium heat until the tomatoes have rendered their juice and most of the liquid has evaporated — about 20 minutes. Work the mixture through a food mill or sieve and set it aside.

Add the penne to 3 quarts of boiling water with 1½ teaspoons of salt. Begin testing the pasta after 10 minutes and cook it until it is *al dente*.

While the pasta is cooking, heat the oil in a large skillet over medium-high heat. Add the onion and sauté it, stirring constantly, until it turns translucent — about three minutes. Add the mushrooms and sauté them for two minutes, then add the bacon and garlic and sauté for two minutes more. Pour in the wine and

cook the mixture until the liquid is reduced by half — about three minutes. Stir in the reserved tomato mixture and the parsley, and keep the sauce warm.

When the penne finishes cooking, transfer it to a platter or bowl. Toss it with the butter and the sauce and serve immediately.

Macaroni Baked with Stilton and Port

Serves 6
Working time: about 20 minutes
Total time: about 45 minutes

Calories **301**
Protein **11g.**
Cholesterol **17mg.**
Total fat **9g.**
Saturated fat **4g.**
Sodium **401mg.**

8 oz. elbow macaroni
1 tbsp. safflower oil
2 shallots, finely chopped
2 tbsp. flour
½ cup ruby Port
1 cup low-fat milk
1 cup unsalted chicken stock
4 oz. Stilton or other blue cheese, crumbled
2 tsp. Dijon mustard
⅛ tsp. white pepper
¼ cup dry bread crumbs
1 tsp. paprika

Preheat the oven to 350° F. Pour the oil into a large, heavy-bottomed saucepan over medium heat. Add the shallots and cook them, stirring occasionally, until they are transparent — approximately two minutes. Sprinkle the flour over the shallots and cook the mixture, stirring continuously, for two minutes more.

Pour the Port into the pan and whisk slowly; add the milk and the stock in the same manner, whisking after each addition, to form a smooth sauce. Gently simmer the sauce for three minutes. Stir in half of the cheese along with the mustard and pepper. Continue stirring until the cheese has melted.

Meanwhile, cook the macaroni in 3 quarts of boiling water with 1½ teaspoons of salt. Start testing the pasta after 10 minutes and cook it until it is *al dente*.

Drain the macaroni and combine it with the sauce, then transfer the mixture to a baking dish. Combine the bread crumbs with the remaining crumbled cheese and scatter the mixture evenly over the top. Sprinkle the paprika over all and bake the dish until the sauce is bubbling hot and the top is crisp — 20 to 25 minutes. Serve immediately.

Rotini with Lemon Sauce and Dill

Serves 4
Working (and total) time: about 20 minutes

Calories **288**
Protein **9g.**
Cholesterol **8mg.**
Total fat **3g.**
Saturated fat **1g.**
Sodium **99mg.**

8 oz. rotini
1 cup milk
⅛ tsp. salt
¼ cup aquavit, or ¼ cup vodka and 1 tsp. caraway seeds
3 tbsp. fresh lemon juice
2-inch strip of lemon zest
2 tbsp. finely cut fresh dill, or 2 tsp. dried dill

Put the milk, salt, aquavit or vodka and caraway seeds, lemon juice and lemon zest in a large nonstick or heavy-bottomed skillet. Bring the liquid to a boil, reduce the heat and simmer gently for three minutes. Add the rotini and enough water to almost cover them. Cover the skillet and cook over low heat, removing the lid and stirring occasionally, until the rotini are *al dente* and about ¼ cup of sauce remains — approximately 15 minutes. (If necessary, add more water to keep the rotini from sticking.) Remove the lemon zest and discard it. Stir in the chopped dill and serve the dish immediately.

Linguine with Mussels in Saffron Sauce

Serves 4
Working (and total) time: about 30 minutes

Calories **474**
Protein **23g.**
Cholesterol **32mg.**
Total fat **8g.**
Saturated fat **2g.**
Sodium **561mg.**

12 oz. linguine
2 lb. large mussels, scrubbed and debearded
1 tbsp. safflower oil
1 shallot, finely chopped
2 tbsp. flour
½ cup dry vermouth
⅛ tsp. saffron threads, steeped in ¾ cup hot water
¼ cup freshly grated Romano cheese
¼ tsp. salt
freshly ground black pepper
1 tbsp. cut chives

Put the mussels and ½ cup of water in a large pan; cover the pan and steam the mussels over high heat until they open — about five minutes. Remove the mussels from the pan with a slotted spoon and set them aside. Discard any mussels that do not open.

When the mussels are cool enough to handle, remove the meat from the shells, working over the pan to catch any liquid; set the meat aside and discard the shells. Strain the liquid left in the bottom of the pan through a very fine sieve. Set the liquid aside.

Heat the safflower oil in a heavy-bottomed skillet over medium-high heat. Add the shallot and sauté it for 30 seconds. Remove the pan from the heat. Whisk in the flour, then the vermouth and the saffron liquid (whisking prevents lumps from forming). Return the

skillet to the heat and simmer the sauce over medium-low heat until it thickens — two to three minutes.

Meanwhile, cook the linguine in 3 quarts of boiling water with 1½ teaspoons of salt. Start testing the pasta after 10 minutes and cook it until it is *al dente*.

To finish the sauce, stir in ¼ cup of the strained mussel-cooking liquid along with the cheese, salt, pepper, chives and mussels. Simmer the sauce for three or four minutes more to heat the mussels through.

Drain the linguine, transfer it to a bowl and toss it with the sauce. Serve immediately.

Linguine Sauced with Capers, Black Olives and Tomatoes

Serves 4
Working (and total) time: about 35 minutes

Calories **302**
Protein **10g.**
Cholesterol **4mg.**
Total fat **6g.**
Saturated fat **1g.**
Sodium **484mg.**

8 oz. linguine
1 garlic clove, very finely chopped
1 tbsp. safflower oil
2½ lb. ripe tomatoes, peeled, seeded and chopped, or 28 oz. canned unsalted whole tomatoes, drained and chopped
2 tsp. capers, drained and chopped
6 oil-cured olives, pitted and cut lengthwise into strips
⅛ tsp. crushed red pepper
¼ tsp. salt
1 tsp. chopped fresh oregano, or ½ tsp. dried oregano
2 tbsp. freshly grated Romano cheese

In a large, heavy-bottomed skillet over medium heat, cook the garlic in the oil for 30 seconds. Add the tomatoes, capers, olives, crushed red pepper and salt. Reduce the heat to low, partially cover the skillet and cook the mixture for 20 minutes. Add the oregano and cook for 10 minutes more.

About 10 minutes before the sauce finishes cooking, add the linguine to 3 quarts of boiling water with 1½ teaspoons of salt. Start testing the linguine after 10 minutes and cook it until it is *al dente.* Drain the pasta and add it to the sauce. Mix well to coat the pasta with the sauce. Sprinkle the cheese on top before serving.

Shells Stuffed with Crab Meat and Spinach

Serves 6
Working time: about 30 minutes
Total time: about 45 minutes

Calories **220**
Protein **14g.**
Cholesterol **52mg.**
Total fat **8g.**
Saturated fat **2g.**
Sodium **366mg.**

12 jumbo pasta shells, each about 2¼ inches long
2 tbsp. safflower oil
1 large onion, chopped (about 1¼ cups)
⅛ tsp. salt
freshly ground black pepper
¼ lb. fresh spinach, stemmed, washed and sliced into a chiffonade
1 tbsp. chopped fresh basil or Italian parsley
2 tbsp. fresh lime juice
12 oz. fresh crab meat, picked over and flaked
½ cup part-skim ricotta

White-wine sauce

½ cup dry white wine
1 tbsp. finely chopped shallot
⅛ tsp. salt
freshly ground black pepper
1 tbsp. chopped fresh basil or Italian parsley
1 tbsp. heavy cream

Preheat the oven to 350° F. Cook the shells in 4 quarts of boiling water with 1 teaspoon of salt, stirring gently to prevent sticking, for 12 minutes — they will be slightly undercooked. Drain the shells and rinse them under cold running water.

While the pasta is cooking, heat 1 tablespoon of the oil in a heavy-bottomed skillet over medium heat. Add the onion, salt and pepper, and cook, stirring frequently, until the onion begins to brown — about 10 minutes. Stir in the spinach, the basil or parsley, and 1 tablespoon of the lime juice. Cook the mixture, stirring, until the spinach wilts — about two minutes.

Remove the skillet from the heat. Add the crab meat, ricotta, the remaining tablespoon of lime juice and some more pepper; mix lightly.

Stuff each shell with some of the crab-meat mixture, gently pressing it down to round out the shell.

Put the shells in a shallow baking dish and drizzle the remaining tablespoon of oil over them. Cover the shells loosely with aluminum foil, shiny side down, and bake them for 20 minutes.

While the shells are baking, prepare the sauce. Put the white wine, shallot, salt, pepper and ½ cup of water in a small saucepan. Bring the mixture to a boil, then reduce the heat to medium low and simmer until only about ⅓ cup of liquid remains — 12 to 15 minutes. Remove the pan from the heat; add the basil or parsley, and whisk in the cream. Return the pan to the heat and cook the sauce for two to three minutes more to thicken it slightly.

Pour the sauce over the baked shells and serve.

EDITOR'S NOTE: *To compensate for shells that may tear during cooking, add one or two extra shells to the boiling water.*

Orzo and Wild Mushrooms

Serves 4 as an appetizer or side dish
Working time: about 30 minutes
Total time: about 40 minutes

Calories **256**
Protein **8g.**
Cholesterol **8mg.**
Total fat **4g.**
Saturated fat **2g.**
Sodium **164mg.**

1 cup orzo
1 oz. dried wild mushrooms (porcini, shiitake or Asian), soaked in 1 cup hot water for 20 minutes
1 tablespoon unsalted butter
1½ cups unsalted chicken stock
1 garlic clove, finely chopped
1 tsp. fresh thyme, or ¼ tsp. dried thyme leaves
¼ tsp. salt
freshly ground black pepper

Remove the mushrooms from their soaking liquid and slice them into thin strips. Strain the soaking liquid through a fine-meshed sieve and reserve ½ cup of it.

Melt the butter in a heavy-bottomed saucepan over medium heat. Add the orzo and the sliced mushrooms to the pan and cook the mixture for five minutes, stirring frequently. Add the reserved mushroom-soaking liquid, ½ cup of the stock, the garlic, thyme, salt and pepper. Cook, stirring all the while, until the orzo has absorbed most of the liquid — seven to eight minutes.

Reduce the heat to low and pour in another ½ cup of stock; cook, stirring constantly, until the liquid has been absorbed — three to four minutes. Repeat this process with the final ½ cup of stock, cooking the mixture until the orzo is tender but still moist. Serve the dish immediately.

Star-Stuffed Peppers

Serves 4
Working time: about 45 minutes
Total time: about 1 hour and 15 minutes

Calories **379**
Protein **17g.**
Cholesterol **23mg.**
Total fat **10g.**
Saturated fat **1g.**
Sodium **350mg.**

1¼ cups stellette (stars)
1 large chicken breast half, skinned and boned (about 5 oz.), the meat cut into small pieces
3 scallions, trimmed and thinly sliced
1 large garlic clove, crushed
1½ tbsp. coarsely chopped fresh ginger
2 tbsp. safflower oil
3 oz. jar pimientos, drained and finely chopped
freshly ground black pepper
2 tsp. white vinegar
½ tsp. salt
4 peppers suitable for stuffing, preferably Anaheim
1 tsp. dark sesame oil

To prepare the stuffing, mound the chicken pieces, scallions, garlic and ginger together on a cutting board and chop them into fine pieces.

Heat the safflower oil in a large, heavy-bottomed skillet over medium heat. Add the chicken mixture to the skillet; sauté the mixture, breaking it up and turning it frequently with a spatula or wooden spoon, until the meat has turned white — about four minutes. Stir in the chopped pimientos, black pepper, vinegar and ¼ teaspoon of the salt.

Add the stars to 2 quarts of boiling water with ½ teaspoon of salt. Start testing them after two minutes and cook them until they are *al dente*. Drain the stars and stir them into the chicken mixture.

Preheat the oven to 350° F. Slice off the peppers' tops and set them aside; with a small spoon, scoop the seeds and the ribs from inside the cavities. Dip a finger into the sesame oil and rub it over the insides of the peppers, then sprinkle the insides with the remaining ¼ teaspoon of salt. Fill the peppers with the chicken stuffing and replace their tops; reserve the stuffing that is left over.

Lightly oil a shallow baking dish and arrange the stuffed peppers in it in a single layer. Bake the peppers for 25 minutes. Remove the dish from the oven and distribute the reserved stuffing around the peppers. Return the dish to the oven for five minutes before serving the peppers.

Fusilli with Chanterelles

Serves 2
Working (and total) time: about 25 minutes

Calories **362**
Protein **10g.**
Cholesterol **15mg.**
Total fat **14g.**
Saturated fat **5g.**
Sodium **382mg.**

4 oz. fusilli (or fettuccine or other narrow ribbon pasta)
1 ripe tomato
1 tbsp. virgin olive oil
1 tbsp. unsalted butter
⅓ lb. chanterelles or oyster mushrooms (pleurotes), wiped clean, trimmed and thinly sliced
¼ tsp. salt
freshly ground black pepper
1 garlic clove, finely chopped
1½ tbsp. finely cut chives or scallions

Place the tomato on a cutting surface with its stem end down. With a sharp knife, cut wide pieces of flesh from the tomato, discarding the seeds and juices. Slice each piece of flesh into very thin strips and set them aside.

Cook the fusilli in 2 quarts of boiling water with 1 teaspoon of salt. Start testing the pasta after 10 minutes and cook it until it is *al dente*.

While the pasta is cooking, heat the oil and butter in a large, heavy-bottomed skillet over medium heat. Add the chanterelles or oyster mushrooms, the ¼ teaspoon of salt and some pepper, and sauté them for three minutes, stirring occasionally. Add the garlic, 1 tablespoon of the chives or scallions, and the tomato. Sauté for two minutes more.

Drain the pasta, add it to the skillet with the mushroom mixture, and toss well. Serve the dish immediately, garnished with the remaining ½ tablespoon of chives or scallions.

Orzo and Mussels

Serves 4
Working time: about 30 minutes
Total time: about 40 minutes

Calories **398**
Protein **17g.**
Cholesterol **19mg.**
Total fat **9g.**
Saturated fat **1g.**
Sodium **391mg.**

8 oz. orzo (or other small pasta)
1 orange
2 tbsp. virgin olive oil
1 onion, finely chopped
4 garlic cloves, finely chopped
2 lb. tomatoes, peeled, seeded and finely chopped (about 2½ cups)
2 tsp. fennel seeds
1½ tbsp. tomato paste
½ cup dry vermouth
¼ tsp. salt
3 tbsp. chopped fresh parsley, or 1 tbsp. dried parsley
1 tsp. fresh thyme, or ¼ tsp. dried thyme leaves
1½ lb. mussels, scrubbed and debearded

With a sharp knife, pare the zest from the orange and cut it into tiny julienne. Put the strips in a small saucepan with 1 cup of cold water. Bring the water to a boil, then remove the pan from the heat. Rinse the zest under cold running water and set it aside. Squeeze the juice from the orange and reserve it as well.

Heat the oil in a large casserole over medium heat. Add the onion and cook it for three minutes, stirring constantly. Add the garlic and cook, stirring, until the onion is translucent — about two minutes more.

Push the onion-garlic mixture to one side of the casserole. Add the tomatoes and the fennel seeds, and raise the heat to high. Cook the tomatoes just enough to soften them without destroying their texture — approximately one minute. Stir the onion-garlic mixture in with the tomatoes. Add the tomato paste, orange juice, vermouth and salt to the casserole, and stir well. Reduce the heat to medium and simmer the sauce for five minutes. Add the parsley, thyme and orange zest.

Place the mussels on top of the sauce. Cover the casserole and steam the mussels until they open — three to five minutes. If any mussels remain closed, discard them. Remove the casserole from the heat and set it aside with its lid on to keep the contents warm.

Add the orzo to three quarts of boiling water with 1½ teaspoons of salt. Start testing after 10 minutes and cook it until it is *al dente*. Drain the orzo and divide it among four deep plates. Ladle the mussels and sauce over each serving.

Gemelli with Sun-Dried Tomatoes, Rosemary and Thyme

Serves 8 as an appetizer
Working time: about 25 minutes
Total time: about 30 minutes

Calories **176**
Protein **5g.**
Cholesterol **2mg.**
Total fat **6g.**
Saturated fat **1g.**
Sodium **248mg.**

8 oz. gemelli (or other short tubular pasta)
2 oz. sun-dried tomatoes packed in oil, drained and thinly sliced
4 small leeks, trimmed, cleaned and cut into ¾-inch slices
2 shallots, finely chopped
1 tsp. fresh rosemary, or ¼ tsp. dried rosemary
1½ tbsp. fresh lemon juice
2 tbsp. virgin olive oil
½ tsp. salt
freshly ground black pepper
1 tsp. fresh thyme, or ¼ tsp. dried thyme leaves
¼ cup dry white wine
¼ cup freshly grated Parmesan cheese

Precook the gemelli in 3 quarts of unsalted boiling water for two minutes — the pasta will be underdone. Drain it and put it in a large casserole. Stir in the toma-toes, 1 cup of water, ½ cup of the white part of the leeks, the shallots, rosemary, lemon juice, 1 table-spoon of the oil, ¼ teaspoon of the salt and some pepper. Cover the casserole and cook the mixture over low heat, stirring occasionally, until all the liquid has been absorbed — about eight minutes.

Meanwhile, in a large, heavy-bottomed skillet, heat the remaining tablespoon of oil over medium heat. Add the remaining leek slices, the remaining ¼ tea-spoon of salt, some pepper and the thyme. Cook the mixture for three minutes, stirring from time to time. Raise the heat to high and cook the mixture for one minute more, then pour in the wine. Cook until the liquid has evaporated — about four minutes.

Add the leek mixture to the casserole, then stir in the cheese. To infuse the pasta with the flavors of the herbs and sun-dried tomatoes, cover the casserole and let it stand for five minutes before serving it.

EDITOR'S NOTE: *Two tablespoons of the oil in which the sun-dried tomatoes are packed may be substituted for the virgin olive oil called for here.*

Vermicelli with Tomatoes and Clams

BEFORE STEAMING THE CLAMS, DISCARD ANY THAT
FAIL TO CLOSE WHEN THEY ARE TAPPED.

Serves 4
Working (and total) time: about 1 hour

Calories **454**
Protein **24g.**
Cholesterol **53mg.**
Total fat **11g.**
Saturated fat **3g.**
Sodium **152mg.**

8 oz. vermicelli or thin spaghetti
36 small hard-shell clams, the shells scrubbed
⅓ cup red wine
5 parsley sprigs
6 garlic cloves, finely chopped
1½ tbsp. virgin olive oil
1 small carrot, peeled and thinly sliced
1 onion, finely chopped
4 lb. ripe tomatoes, peeled, seeded and chopped, or 48 oz. unsalted canned whole tomatoes, drained and chopped
2 tsp. finely chopped fresh oregano, or 1 tsp. dried oregano
1½ tsp. finely chopped fresh thyme, or ½ tsp. dried thyme leaves
freshly ground black pepper
1 tbsp. unsalted butter

In a large pot, combine the clams, wine, parsley and half of the garlic. Cover the pot tightly and steam the clams over medium-high heat for five minutes. Transfer to a bowl any clams that have opened. Re-cover the pot and steam the remaining clams for about three minutes more. Again, transfer the opened clams to the bowl; discard any clams that are still closed. Strain the wine mixture remaining in the pot through a very fine sieve and reserve ⅓ cup of it for the sauce. When the clams are cool enough to handle, remove them from their shells and reserve them along with any liquid remaining in the bowl.

To make the sauce, pour the oil into a heavy-bottomed saucepan over medium heat. Add the carrot and onion, and sauté them until the onion is translucent — about five minutes. Add the remaining garlic and cook the mixture for three minutes more. Stir in the tomatoes, oregano and thyme. Reduce the heat to low and continue cooking, stirring often, until the sauce is quite thick — about 15 minutes. Then add the clams to the sauce, along with their liquid and the reserved wine mixture. Stir in a generous amount of black pepper.

About 5 minutes after adding the tomatoes to the sauce, put the vermicelli into 3 quarts of boiling water with 1½ teaspoons of salt. Start testing the vermicelli after six minutes and cook it until it is *al dente.*

Drain the vermicelli and return it to the cooking pot; add the butter and toss well to coat the pasta. Pour the clam sauce over the pasta and serve at once.

Ditalini Gratin
with Jalapeño Pepper

IN THIS DISH, PASTA AND SAUCE ARE COOKED TOGETHER,
WITH THE STARCH IN THE PASTA SERVING AS THE THICKENING
AGENT FOR THE SAUCE.

Serves 6 as a side dish
Working time: about 25 minutes
Total time: about 30 minutes

Calories **226**
Protein **10g.**
Cholesterol **12mg.**
Total fat **4g.**
Saturated fat **3g.**
Sodium **183mg.**

8 oz. ditalini (or other small, tubular pasta)
1½ lb. ripe tomatoes, peeled, seeded and chopped, or 14 oz. unsalted canned whole tomatoes, drained and chopped
1 onion, chopped
1 cup low-fat milk
1 jalapeño pepper, seeded, deribbed and finely chopped (caution, page 33)
1 garlic clove, finely chopped
¼ tsp. ground cumin
¼ tsp. salt
freshly ground black pepper
2 oz. Monterey Jack cheese, finely diced

Put the tomatoes, onion and milk in a large, heavy-bottomed skillet, and bring the mixture to a boil. Add the ditalini, jalapeño pepper, garlic, cumin, salt and a liberal grinding of pepper. Stir to mix thoroughly, then cover the pan and reduce the heat to medium. Simmer the mixture for two minutes, stirring from time to time to keep the pasta from sticking to the bottom. Preheat the broiler.

Pour into the skillet just enough water to cover the ditalini. Cook the pasta, removing the lid frequently to stir the mixture and keep it covered with liquid, until the pasta is just tender and a creamy sauce has formed — about seven minutes.

Transfer the contents of the skillet to a gratin dish. Sprinkle the cheese over the top and broil the pasta until the cheese is melted — two to three minutes. Serve the dish immediately.

Fettuccine with Broiled Eggplant

Serves 4
Working time: about 30 minutes
Total time: about 40 minutes

Calories **353**
Protein **9g.**
Cholesterol **0mg.**
Total fat **13g.**
Saturated fat **1g.**
Sodium **237mg.**

8 oz. fettuccine (or other narrow ribbon pasta)
1 medium eggplant (about 1 lb.), cut lengthwise into 1-inch-thick slices
2½ tbsp. virgin olive oil
1 large, ripe tomato, peeled and seeded
½ cup oil-packed sun-dried tomatoes (about 1¾ oz.), drained and thinly sliced
1 shallot, finely chopped
1 garlic clove, finely chopped
1 tbsp. red wine vinegar
freshly ground black pepper
¼ cup chopped fresh basil

Preheat the broiler. Brush both sides of the eggplant slices with 1½ tablespoons of the oil. Cut each eggplant slice into cubes. Put the eggplant cubes on a baking sheet in a single layer, then broil them until they are well browned on one side. Turn the pieces over and broil once more until brown. Turn off the broiler, but leave the eggplant in the oven to keep it warm.

Cook the fettuccine in 3 quarts of boiling water with 1½ teaspoons of salt; start testing the pasta after 10 minutes and cook it until it is *al dente*.

Purée the fresh tomato in a food processor or blender. Put the tomato purée in a small saucepan along with the sun-dried tomatoes, shallot, garlic, vinegar, the remaining tablespoon of oil and a generous grind-

ing of pepper. Place the pan over low heat, bring the mixture to a simmer, and cook it for two minutes. Remove the pan from the heat and stir in the basil.

When the pasta finishes cooking, drain it and transfer it to a large serving bowl. Add the warm eggplant cubes and the sauce, toss well, and serve at once.

EDITOR'S NOTE: *Two and one half tablespoons of the olive or sunflower oil in which the sun-dried tomatoes are packed may be substituted for the virgin olive oil called for here.*

Vermicelli with Shrimp and Fennel

Serves 6
Working time: about 35 minutes
Total time: about 45 minutes

Calories **366**
Protein **17g.**
Cholesterol **85mg.**
Total fat **12g.**
Saturated fat **4g.**
Sodium **227mg.**

12 oz. vermicelli (or other thin spaghetti)
⅔ lb. large fresh shrimp, peeled, deveined and halved lengthwise
½ tsp. fennel seeds (optional), crushed with a mortar and pestle
4 shallots, thinly sliced
2 garlic cloves, very finely chopped
freshly ground black pepper
2 tbsp. virgin olive oil
1 lemon, cut in half
2 fennel bulbs (about ⅔ lb.), stalks and green feathery tops reserved for another use, the bulbs very thinly sliced
3 tbsp. unsalted butter
¼ cup dry bread crumbs

Put the shrimp, fennel seeds if you are using them, shallot and garlic in a bowl. Grind in plenty of black pepper, then add 1 tablespoon of the oil and mix well. Squeeze the juice of one lemon half into the bowl, mix well again, and set the bowl aside. Put the fennel slices in a separate small bowl and squeeze the juice of the remaining lemon half over them.

Heat the remaining tablespoon of oil in a large skillet over high heat. When the oil is hot, add the fennel slices and sauté them, stirring constantly, for five minutes. Add the shrimp mixture and cook just until the shrimp turn pink — about two minutes. Transfer the contents of the skillet to a serving bowl and set the bowl aside in a warm place.

Return the skillet to the stove and reduce the heat to low. Melt the butter in the skillet. Add the bread crumbs and cook them, stirring often, until they are crisp and golden brown — about four minutes.

While the bread crumbs are browning, add the vermicelli to 3 quarts of boiling water with 1½ teaspoons of salt. Cook the pasta until it is *al dente* — about four minutes. Drain the pasta, add it to the shrimp-and-fennel mixture, and toss well. Scatter the bread crumbs over the pasta and serve immediately.

Manicotti Stuffed with Turkey, Kale and Cheese

Serves 6
Working time: about 30 minutes
Total time: about 2 hours

Calories **449**
Protein **38g.**
Cholesterol **70mg.**
Total fat **12g.**
Saturated fat **7g.**
Sodium **472mg.**

12 manicotti tubes (about 8 oz.)
1 lb. turkey breast meat, cut into 1-inch cubes
1 small onion, finely chopped
½ tsp. fresh thyme, or ¼ tsp. dried thyme leaves
¼ cup dry vermouth
2 cups unsalted chicken stock
1 cup low-fat ricotta cheese
1 cup low-fat cottage cheese
6 tbsp. freshly grated Parmesan cheese
½ lb. kale, cooked, thoroughly drained and finely chopped
freshly ground black pepper
grated nutmeg
2 tbsp. unsalted butter
4 tbsp. all-purpose flour
2 cups skim milk

To begin making the stuffing, combine the turkey cubes, onion, thyme and vermouth in a bowl. Allow the cubes to marinate for at least 30 minutes.

Strain the marinade into a large, nonreactive skillet over medium heat. Pour in the stock and bring the liquid to a simmer. Add the turkey cubes and poach them until they are no longer pink at the center — about four minutes.

With a slotted spoon, transfer the cubes to a food processor, reserving their poaching liquid. Operate the machine in short bursts until the cubes are finely chopped. Add the ricotta, the cottage cheese, 4 tablespoons of the Parmesan and the kale, and mix. Season the mixture with pepper and nutmeg, and set it aside.

To prepare the sauce, melt the butter in a 2-quart saucepan over medium heat. Gradually whisk in the flour to make a paste and cook for two minutes. Add the reserved poaching liquid and bring the mixture to a boil, whisking constantly to prevent lumps from forming. Pour in the milk and return the liquid to a boil, whisking frequently. Reduce the heat to low and let the sauce simmer gently for about 15 minutes while you prepare the manicotti.

Add the manicotti to 4 quarts of boiling water with 2 teaspoons of salt. Start testing the pasta after 15 minutes and cook it until it is *al dente*. When the manicotti are done, transfer them to a bowl of cold water.

Preheat the oven to 400° F. Thoroughly drain the manicotti tubes and stuff each one carefully with the turkey mixture.

Arrange the manicotti in a single layer in a large baking dish. Ladle the sauce over the manicotti and sprinkle the remaining 2 tablespoons of Parmesan cheese over the top. Cover the dish with aluminum foil and bake it until the sauce bubbles and the pasta is heated through — about 30 minutes. Remove the foil from the dish and brown the manicotti under the broiler for about five minutes. Serve immediately.

EDITOR'S NOTE: *To allow for manicotti tubes that may tear during cooking or while being stuffed, add one or two extra tubes to the boiling water. The manicotti may be assembled in advance and refrigerated for up to 24 hours before the sauce and Parmesan cheese are added and the dish is baked.*

Mafalda with Lobster, Collard Greens and Brown Butter

Serves 2
Working time: about 30 minutes
Total time: about 1 hour

Calories **428**
Protein **25g.**
Cholesterol **106mg.**
Total fat **15g.**
Saturated fat **7g.**
Sodium **425mg.**

4 oz. mafalda (or other curly-edged ribbon pasta)
1 live lobster (about 1¼ lb.)
1 lemon or lime, cut in half
½ lb. collard greens, washed, stemmed and cut into ½-inch-wide strips
2 tbsp. unsalted butter
freshly ground black pepper

Pour enough water into a large pot to fill it to a depth of about 1 inch. Bring the water to a boil and add the lobster. Cover the pot tightly and steam the lobster until it turns a bright reddish orange — about 10 minutes. Remove the lobster from the pot and set it on a dish to catch the juices; do not discard the cooking liquid. Pour 2 quarts of water into the pot and bring the liquid to a boil.

Holding the lobster over the dish, remove the tail by twisting it away from the body. Twist the claws off the body, then crack the shell of the tail and claws. Remove the meat and slice it thinly. Add the shells and lobster juices to the pot with the boiling liquid. Allow the shells to boil for 10 minutes. With a slotted spoon, remove the shells and discard them. Squeeze the juice of one of the lemon or lime halves into the liquid. Add the mafalda and cover the pot. When the liquid returns to a boil, remove the lid. Start testing the pasta after 11 minutes and cook it until it is *al dente*.

While the pasta is cooking, transfer ⅓ cup of the cooking liquid to a large, heavy-bottomed skillet and bring it to a simmer. Add the collard greens and cook them, stirring occasionally, until all of the liquid has evaporated and the greens are completely wilted. Melt the butter in a small, heavy-bottomed saucepan over medium heat and cook it just until it turns nut brown; watch the butter carefully after it stops bubbling lest it burn. Scatter the lobster meat over the collard greens in the skillet. Squeeze the juice of the remaining lemon or lime half over the lobster.

When the pasta finishes cooking, drain it and add it to the skillet. Add some pepper, pour the butter over the pasta, and toss well. Serve immediately.

Linguine and Chilied Shrimp

Serves 4
Working time: about 20 minutes
Total time: about 1 hour

Calories **495**
Protein **23g.**
Cholesterol **133mg.**
Total fat **20g.**
Saturated fat **6g.**
Sodium **390mg.**

8 oz. linguine
3 tbsp. unsalted butter
1 onion, finely chopped (about 1 cup)
12 oz. beer
1 bay leaf
2 tbsp. safflower oil
1 lb. fresh shrimp, peeled and deveined, the shells reserved
1 garlic clove, finely chopped
1 tbsp. chili powder
¼ tsp. salt
freshly ground black pepper
⅓ avocado, peeled and thinly sliced

To make the sauce, melt the butter in a saucepan over medium-high heat. Add the onion and cook it until it is translucent — about two minutes. Add the beer, bay leaf and reserved shrimp shells, and bring the liquid to a simmer. Reduce the heat to low, cover the pan, and simmer the mixture for 20 minutes.

Add the linguine to 3 quarts of boiling water with 1½ teaspoons of salt. After eight minutes, drain the pasta and set it aside; it will be slightly underdone.

Strain the shrimp-shell liquid, discarding the solids, and return the liquid to the pan; there will be a little more than a cup. Add the reserved linguine to the liquid and simmer it, covered, until it is *al dente* — about four minutes.

While the pasta finishes cooking, pour the oil into a large, heavy-bottomed skillet over medium-high heat. Add the shrimp and sauté them, stirring occasionally, until they become firm and opaque — one to two minutes. Stir in the garlic and cook for 30 seconds more. Season the shrimp with the chili powder, the ¼ teaspoon of salt and some pepper.

Add the avocado to the linguine and toss. Transfer the mixture to a platter, arrange the shrimp on top of the pasta, and serve hot.

Linguine and Chicken in Parsley Sauce

Serves 4
Working time: about 25 minutes
Total time: about 30 minutes

Calories **398**
Protein **23g.**
Cholesterol **52mg.**
Total fat **13g.**
Saturated fat **5g.**
Sodium **307mg.**

8 oz. linguine
1 tbsp. safflower oil
zest of 1 lemon, finely julienned
1 tsp. finely chopped fresh ginger
1 tsp. sugar
¼ tsp. salt
1 cup unsalted chicken stock
2 tbsp. unsalted butter
2 chicken breast halves, skinned and boned (about 8 oz.), cut into ¾-inch cubes
2 shallots, finely chopped
2 bunches of parsley, stemmed (about 3 cups)

Cook the oil and lemon zest in a saucepan over medium heat for four minutes. Stir in the ginger, sugar and ⅛ teaspoon of the salt, and cook the mixture for three minutes more, stirring frequently. Pour in the stock and bring the mixture to a boil; cook it until only about ½ cup of liquid remains — five to seven minutes.

Cook the linguine in 3 quarts of boiling water with 1½ teaspoons of salt. Start testing the pasta after 10 minutes and cook it until it is *al dente*.

While the pasta is cooking, melt 1 tablespoon of the butter in a large, heavy-bottomed skillet over medium-high heat. Add the chicken cubes and shallots; sauté them, stirring frequently, until the cubes are lightly browned — about three minutes. Stir in the lemon-zest mixture and cook for one minute more. Add the parsley and cook, stirring, for an additional three minutes.

Drain the pasta and transfer it to a casserole. Stir the remaining tablespoon of butter into the sauce and combine the sauce with the pasta. Cover the casserole and let the dish stand for five minutes, stirring once, to meld the flavors.

Rotini with Liver, Onions and Sugar Snap Peas

Serves 4
Working (and total) time: about 35 minutes

Calories **376**
Protein **15g.**
Cholesterol **132mg.**
Total fat **12g.**
Saturated fat **3g.**
Sodium **264mg.**

8 oz. rotini (or other short pasta)
2 tbsp. virgin olive oil
4 oz. chicken livers (about ½ cup), trimmed and cut into ½-inch pieces
¼ tsp. salt
2 onions, thinly sliced
¼ cup cider vinegar
1 tbsp. unsalted butter
½ lb. small sugar snap peas or snow peas, stems and strings removed
freshly ground black pepper

Heat 1 tablespoon of the oil in a large, nonstick or heavy-bottomed skillet over medium-high heat. Sauté the chicken-liver pieces, stirring constantly, until they turn brown — 30 to 45 seconds. Sprinkle the liver pieces with ⅛ teaspoon of the salt, remove them from the pan and set them aside.

Return the skillet to the heat without washing it and add the remaining tablespoon of oil. Add the onions and vinegar, and stir to deglaze the pan. Cook, stirring frequently, until the onions are golden brown — about 15 minutes.

Meanwhile, cook the pasta in 3 quarts of boiling water with 1½ teaspoons of salt. Begin testing the pasta after 8 minutes and cook it until it is *al dente*.

While the pasta is cooking, melt the butter in a skillet over medium heat. Add the peas and cook them until they are tender — about seven minutes. Sprinkle the peas with the remaining ⅛ teaspoon of salt and some pepper. Drain the pasta and add it to the skillet with the onions. Add the reserved liver pieces and peas, toss thoroughly, and serve immediately.

Spaghetti with Smoked Salmon and Watercress

Serves 4
Working (and total) time: about 15 minutes

Calories **243**
Protein **10g.**
Cholesterol **3mg.**
Total fat **3g.**
Saturated fat **0g.**
Sodium **216mg.**

8 oz. spaghetti
1½ tsp. virgin olive oil
1 garlic clove, finely chopped
2 oz. smoked salmon, julienned
1 bunch watercress, washed and stemmed
freshly ground black pepper

Cook the spaghetti in 3 quarts of boiling water with 1½ teaspoons of salt. Start testing the pasta after eight minutes and cook it until it is *al dente*.

Just before the spaghetti finishes cooking, heat the oil in a large skillet over medium heat. Cook the garlic in the oil for 30 seconds, stirring constantly. Add the salmon, watercress and pepper, and cook for 30 seconds more before removing the skillet from the heat.

Drain the spaghetti and add it to the skillet. Toss the spaghetti to distribute the sauce and serve at once.

Farfalle in Red-Pepper Sauce with Broccoli

Serves 4
Working time: about 15 minutes
Total time: about 25 minutes

Calories **285**
Protein **11g.**
Cholesterol **4mg.**
Total fat **6g.**
Saturated fat **2g.**
Sodium **352mg.**

8 oz. farfalle (or other fancy-shaped pasta)
1 tbsp. virgin olive oil
1 garlic clove, finely chopped
2 red peppers, seeded, deribbed and coarsely chopped
¼ tsp. salt
1 cup unsalted chicken stock
1 cup broccoli florets, blanched in boiling water for 2 minutes and refreshed under cold running water
1 tbsp. chopped fresh basil, or 1 tsp. dried basil
½ tbsp. chopped fresh oregano, or ½ tsp. dried oregano
freshly ground black pepper
¼ cup freshly grated Parmesan cheese

Heat the oil in a large, heavy-bottomed skillet over medium heat. Add the garlic and cook it for 30 seconds, stirring constantly. Add the chopped red peppers, salt and chicken stock. Simmer the mixture until only ⅓ cup of liquid remains — seven to eight minutes.

Meanwhile, cook the farfalle in 3 quarts of boiling water with 1½ teaspoons of salt. Start testing the pasta after eight minutes and cook it until it is *al dente*. Drain the pasta and transfer it to a bowl.

Purée the red-pepper mixture in a blender or food processor. Strain the sauce through a sieve back into the skillet. Stir in the broccoli, basil, oregano, pepper and cheese. Simmer the sauce until the broccoli is heated through — two to three minutes. Toss the farfalle with the sauce and serve immediately.

Pasta Shells and Scallops

Serves 6
Working (and total) time: about 25 minutes

Calories **299**
Protein **18g.**
Cholesterol **42mg.**
Total fat **9g.**
Saturated fat **4g.**
Sodium **460mg.**

8 oz. medium pasta shells
1 tbsp. safflower oil
1 small onion, finely chopped (about 1 cup)
2 tbsp. flour
1½ cups unsalted chicken or fish stock
¼ cup heavy cream
⅛ tsp. grated nutmeg
¼ tsp. salt
¼ tsp. white pepper
¾ lb. sea scallops, the connective muscle at their sides removed, as necessary
¼ cup fresh bread crumbs
½ cup freshly grated Parmesan cheese
¼ tsp. paprika
parsley sprigs for garnish

Add the pasta shells to 3 quarts of boiling water with 1½ teaspoons of salt. Start testing the pasta after eight minutes and cook it until it is *al dente*.

Meanwhile, to prepare the sauce, pour the oil into a shallow casserole over medium heat. Add the onion and sauté it until it turns translucent — about three minutes. Stir in the flour and continue to cook, stirring constantly, for two minutes. Remove the casserole from the heat. Slowly whisk in the stock and cream, stirring the mixture until it is smooth. Add the nutmeg, salt and pepper, and stir. Preheat the broiler.

Drain the pasta and add it, along with the scallops, to the sauce. Return the casserole to the stove and bring the sauce to a simmer. Cover the casserole and simmer gently until the scallops become opaque — two or three minutes.

To prepare the dish for the table, wipe any sauce from the visible inside walls of the casserole. Then top the dish with the bread crumbs, cheese and paprika and broil it until the topping is golden — about two minutes. Garnish with the parsley sprigs and serve hot.

Rigatoni with Red Potatoes and Radicchio

Serves 6 as an appetizer
Working (and total) time: about 45 minutes

Calories **273**
Protein **7g.**
Cholesterol **0mg.**
Total fat **10g.**
Saturated fat **1g.**
Sodium **98mg.**

8 oz. rigatoni (or medium shells)
3 large unpeeled red potatoes (about ½ lb.), each cut into 8 pieces
4 tbsp. virgin olive oil
½ lb. spinach, washed, stemmed, and squeezed into a ball to remove excess water
2 garlic cloves, finely chopped
1 small head radicchio (about 4 oz.), torn into 1½-inch pieces
2 tbsp. Dijon mustard
2 tbsp. red wine vinegar
¼ cup chopped fresh basil
2 bunches scallions, trimmed and cut into 1-inch pieces
freshly ground black pepper

In a large, covered pot, bring 3 quarts of water and 1½ teaspoons of salt to a boil; add the rigatoni to the boiling water. Start testing the pasta after 13 minutes and cook it until it is *al dente*.

While the pasta is cooking, pour enough water into a saucepan to fill it about 1 inch deep. Add ½ teaspoon of salt and set a vegetable steamer in the bottom of the pan. Bring the water to a boil. Add the potatoes, cover the pot, and steam the potatoes until they are tender when pierced with the tip of a thin knife — about eight minutes. Transfer the potatoes to a large bowl.

When the pasta is cooked, drain it and transfer it to the bowl with the potatoes. Pour in 1 tablespoon of the oil and toss well to coat the pasta and the potatoes.

Heat another tablespoon of the oil in a large, heavy-bottomed skillet over medium-high heat. When it is hot, add the spinach and garlic, and sauté them for 30 seconds, stirring constantly. Add the radicchio and cook until the spinach has wilted — about 30 seconds more. Scrape the contents of the skillet into the bowl containing the pasta and the potatoes.

In a small bowl, whisk together the mustard and vinegar. Whisk in the remaining 2 tablespoons of oil, then pour this mixture over the pasta. Add the basil, scallions and some pepper to the bowl, toss well to combine, and serve.

EDITOR'S NOTE: *This dish may be served warm, at room temperature, or chilled.*

Capellini with Chilled Tomatoes, Black Olives and Garlic

Serves 6 as an appetizer
Working time: about 20 minutes
Total time: about 1 hour

Calories **190**
Protein **6g.**
Cholesterol **0mg.**
Total fat **4g.**
Saturated fat **0g.**
Sodium **191mg.**

8 oz. capellini (or other thin spaghetti)
3 large, ripe tomatoes, peeled, seeded and chopped (about 2 cups)
4 garlic cloves, finely chopped
5 oil-cured black olives, pitted and finely chopped
1 small hot chili pepper, seeded, deribbed and finely chopped (caution, page 33)
1 tbsp. virgin olive oil
juice of 1 lime
1 tbsp. chopped cilantro
⅛ tsp. salt
freshly ground black pepper

Put the chopped tomatoes in a strainer set over a large bowl; place the bowl in the refrigerator and let the tomatoes drain for at least 30 minutes.

Put 3 quarts of water on to boil with 1½ teaspoons of salt. In a separate bowl, combine the garlic, olives, chili pepper, oil, lime juice, cilantro, salt and pepper. Refrigerate the mixture.

Drop the capellini into the boiling water. Begin testing the pasta after three minutes and continue to cook it until it is *al dente*.

While the pasta is cooking, combine the garlic mixture with the drained tomatoes; discard the juice. Drain the pasta, put it in a bowl and toss it immediately with the sauce.

Cavatappi with Spinach and Ham

Serves 4
Working time: about 25 minutes
Total time: about 35 minutes

Calories **328**
Protein **13g.**
Cholesterol **35mg.**
Total fat **11g.**
Saturated fat **5g.**
Sodium **360mg.**

8 oz. cavatappi (or other short, tubular pasta)
2 tsp. unsalted butter
1 small onion, finely chopped
2 garlic cloves, finely chopped
2 cups unsalted chicken stock
¼ cup dry vermouth
¼ cup heavy cream
1 bay leaf
grated nutmeg
freshly ground black pepper
2 oz. ham, julienned
1 lb. fresh spinach, washed and stemmed

Melt the butter in a large nonreactive skillet over medium-high heat. Add the onion and garlic, and sauté them until they turn translucent — about five minutes. Add the stock, vermouth, cream, bay leaf, a little nutmeg and some pepper, and cook the mixture until it is reduced to about 1 cup — 10 to 15 minutes.

While the stock mixture is reducing, add the pasta to 3 quarts of boiling water with 1½ teaspoons of salt. Start testing the pasta after 10 minutes and cook it until it is *al dente*.

About three minutes before the pasta finishes cooking, remove the bay leaf from the mixture in the skillet and discard it. Stir in the ham and spinach, then cover the skillet and steam the spinach for three minutes. Remove the cover and stir the mixture until the spinach is completely wilted — about 30 seconds. Turn off the heat.

Drain the pasta and immediately stir it into the spinach-and-ham mixture. Allow the pasta mixture to stand for one minute. Stir it again just before serving.

Noodles, Cabbage and Caraway

Serves 6 as a side dish
Working time: about 15 minutes
Total time: about 50 minutes

Calories **167**
Protein **5g.**
Cholesterol **32mg.**
Total fat **4g.**
Saturated fat **2g.**
Sodium **157mg.**

6 oz. wide or extra-wide egg noodles
2 onions, sliced
⅓ cup cider vinegar
1½ tbsp. unsalted butter
¾ tsp. caraway seeds
¼ tsp. salt
½ small cabbage (about ¾ lb.), cored and cut into 1-inch-wide strips
1 tbsp. paprika, preferably Hungarian
1 tsp. dark brown sugar
freshly ground black pepper

Pour ¾ cup of water into a large pot. Add the onions, vinegar, butter, caraway seeds and salt, and bring the mixture to a boil. Cook, stirring frequently, for five minutes. Reduce the heat to medium low, then stir in the cabbage, paprika and brown sugar. Cover the pot and cook for 35 minutes, removing the lid three times to stir. Add water, if necessary, to ensure that the liquid in the pot remains about ½ inch deep.

Approximately five minutes before the cabbage finishes cooking, drop the noodles into 2 quarts of boiling water with 1 teaspoon of salt and cook them for five minutes. The noodles will be undercooked. Drain them and add them to the cabbage mixture along with some pepper. Cook over medium-low heat, stirring occasionally, until all the liquid has evaporated and the noodles are *al dente* — five to seven minutes.

Chicken Couscous with Raisins and Almonds

Serves 6
Working (and total) time: about 1 hour

Calories **336**	1 cup couscous
Protein **31g.**	6 chicken drumsticks, skinned and boned, the meat
Cholesterol **90mg.**	cut into 1-inch pieces
Total fat **13g.**	⅛ tsp. cayenne pepper
Saturated fat **3g.**	¼ tsp. ground cloves
Sodium **188mg.**	¼ tsp. ground cinnamon
	¼ tsp. ground cardamom
	½ tsp. ground cumin
	1 tsp. turmeric
	¼ cup raisins
	1 tbsp. safflower oil
	1 onion, finely chopped
	4 garlic cloves, finely chopped
	¼ tsp. salt
	2 cups unsalted chicken stock
	2 tbsp. slivered almonds

Put the chicken pieces in a bowl and sprinkle them with the cayenne pepper, cloves, cinnamon, cardamom, cumin and turmeric. Toss the pieces to coat them with the spices. Let them stand at room temperature for at least 30 minutes.

To prepare the couscous, combine it with the raisins in a bowl and pour in 1 cup of boiling water. Cover the bowl and let it stand for at least five minutes.

Heat the oil in a large, heavy-bottomed skillet over medium heat, tilting the pan to coat it evenly. Add the onion and garlic and sauté them, stirring constantly, until the onion is translucent — about three minutes. Sprinkle the salt over the chicken and add the pieces to the skillet. Sauté, stirring frequently, until the chicken feels firm but springy to the touch — about five minutes. Pour the stock over the chicken and bring the liquid to a boil. Immediately drain the chicken and onions, reserving the liquid and the solids separately, and set them aside.

Fluff up the couscous-and-raisin mixture with a fork

and transfer it to a serving platter, hollowing out the center to form the couscous into the shape of a wreath. Mound the chicken mixture in the center of the wreath. Drizzle the stock over all and top the dish with the slivered almonds.

Spinach-Shell Salad with Chunks of Chicken

Serves 4
Working (and total) time: about 40 minutes

Calories **319**
Protein **22g.**
Cholesterol **36mg.**
Total fat **3g.**
Saturated fat **1g.**
Sodium **272mg.**

8 oz. medium spinach shells
2 chicken breast halves, skinned and boned (about ½ lb.), cut into pieces about 1 inch square
¼ tsp. salt
freshly ground black pepper
2 large shallots, thinly sliced
½ tsp. ground cinnamon
3 ripe tomatoes (about 1½ lb.), peeled, seeded and chopped
zest of 1 orange, cut into thin strips

Arrange the chicken pieces in a single layer in a deep, heatproof dish or a pie pan about 10 inches in diameter. Sprinkle the chicken with the salt and pepper. Scatter the shallot slices evenly over the chicken and top them with the cinnamon and tomatoes. Strew the orange zest over all. Cover the dish tightly with foil.

Pour enough water into a saucepan approximately 8 inches in diameter to fill it about one third full. Bring the water to a rolling boil. Set the covered dish on top of the saucepan like a lid and cook the chicken over the boiling water. After five minutes, test the chicken: If the meat is still pink at the center, cover the dish again and continue to steam the chicken until all trace of pink has disappeared and the meat feels firm but springy to the touch. Remove the dish from the saucepan and uncover it.

While the chicken is cooking, add the shells to 3 quarts of boiling water with 1½ teaspoons of salt. Start testing the shells after 12 minutes and cook them until they are *al dente*.

Drain the shells and transfer them to a heated bowl. Add the chicken-and-tomato sauce and toss it with the shells. Serve hot or at room temperature.

Couscous Vegetable Salad

Serves 6
Working (and total) time: about 20 minutes

Calories **196**
Protein **9g.**
Cholesterol **6mg.**
Total fat **4g.**
Saturated fat **1g.**
Sodium **285mg.**

8 oz. couscous (about 1½ cups)
1 lb. fresh peas, shelled (about 1 cup), or 1 cup frozen peas
1 tbsp. safflower oil
1 garlic clove, crushed
1 cup fresh corn, cut from 1 large ear, or 1 cup frozen corn
¼ tsp. salt
freshly ground black pepper
1 tsp. finely chopped fresh thyme, or ½ tsp. dried thyme leaves
1 cup unsalted chicken stock
½ tbsp. white wine vinegar
2 oz. lean ham, finely chopped
12 romaine lettuce leaves
Tomato-scallion topping
1 tbsp. white wine vinegar
1 small chili pepper, seeded, deribbed and coarsely chopped (caution, page 33)
1 large tomato, peeled, seeded and finely chopped
2 scallions, trimmed and finely chopped
1 tbsp. finely chopped fresh basil, or ½ tbsp. dried basil

Put the couscous in a 1-quart bowl and pour 1 cup of boiling water over it. Cover the bowl and let it stand undisturbed until the couscous has completely absorbed the water — about five minutes.

If you are using fresh peas, parboil them until they are barely tender — three to four minutes — then drain them and refresh them under cold running water.

Heat the oil in a large, heavy-bottomed skillet or flameproof casserole over medium heat. Add the garlic and cook it for about 30 seconds. Stir in the peas and corn along with the salt, pepper, thyme and stock. Bring the mixture to a simmer and cook it until the liquid is reduced by one third — about five minutes.

Meanwhile, sprinkle the ½ tablespoon of vinegar over the couscous, then add the ham. Combine the reduced stock mixture with the couscous and stir well.

To prepare the topping, pour the tablespoon of vinegar into a small bowl with the chili pepper. Let the combination stand for five minutes to allow the vinegar to mellow the pepper's hotness, then stir in the tomato, scallions and basil.

Arrange two lettuce leaves on each of six individual plates. (Alternatively, arrange all of the lettuce leaves on a large serving platter.) Mound the couscous salad on the lettuce leaves, then spread the topping over the couscous. The dish may be served chilled or at room temperature.

Egg Noodles with Carrots, Snow Peas and Lamb

THIS DISH MAY BE SERVED WARM OR COLD.

Serves 4
Working (and total) time: about 40 minutes

Calories **502**
Protein **20g.**
Cholesterol **83mg.**
Total fat **23g.**
Saturated fat **10g.**
Sodium **295mg.**

8 oz. fine egg noodles
2 tsp. honey
2 tbsp. lime juice
1½ tsp. curry powder
2 tbsp. virgin olive oil
½ lb. lean boneless lamb, cut into strips about 1 inch long and ¼ inch wide
1 garlic clove, finely chopped
¼ teaspoon salt
4 scallions, trimmed and thinly sliced, the white and green parts kept separate
½ cup unsalted chicken stock
1 large carrot, peeled, halved lengthwise and sliced diagonally into very thin crescents
¼ lb. snow peas, stems and strings removed, each pod sliced diagonally into thirds

In a small dish, combine the honey, lime juice and curry powder; set the mixture aside. Add the noodles to 3 quarts of boiling water with 1½ teaspoons of salt. Start testing the noodles after five minutes and cook them until they are *al dente*. Drain the noodles, transfer them to a large bowl, and toss them with 1 tablespoon of the oil.

Pour the remaining tablespoon of olive oil into a large, heavy-bottomed skillet over medium-high heat. When the oil is hot, add the lamb and cook it, stirring constantly, for about 30 seconds. Stir in the garlic, ⅛ teaspoon of the salt, the white part of the scallions and the honey mixture. Cook for 30 seconds more, stirring constantly. Scrape the mixture into the bowl with the noodles and toss well. Do not wash the skillet.

Return the skillet to the stove over medium-high heat; pour in the stock, then add the carrot and the remaining ⅛ teaspoon of salt. Cook the mixture, scraping up any caramelized bits, for about three minutes. Add the snow peas and cook for one minute more, stirring all the while. Transfer the mixture to the bowl containing the noodles, add the scallion greens, and mix thoroughly.

Couscous with Spicy Vegetables

Serves 6
Working (and total) time: about 45 minutes

Calories **150**
Protein **6g.**
Cholesterol **0mg.**
Total fat **3g.**
Saturated fat **0g.**
Sodium **90mg.**

1 cup couscous
1 tbsp. safflower oil
6 scallions, trimmed, the white bottoms finely chopped, the green tops cut into ¼-inch pieces
4 garlic cloves, finely chopped
1 tbsp. finely chopped fresh ginger
1 turnip (about ½ lb.), peeled and cut into ½-inch cubes
4 carrots (about ½ lb.), peeled and cut into ½-inch-thick rounds
⅛ tsp. crushed red pepper
⅛ tsp. ground coriander
2 cups unsalted chicken stock
2 zucchini (about ¾ lb.), cut into ½-inch-thick rounds
1 red sweet pepper, stemmed, seeded, deribbed and cut into ½-inch pieces

Put the couscous in a bowl and pour 1 cup of boiling water over it. Cover the bowl and let the couscous stand for at least five minutes.

To prepare the vegetables, heat the oil in a large, deep, heavy-bottomed skillet over medium-high heat. Add the white scallion bottoms, the garlic and ginger, and sauté for one minute, stirring constantly. Add the turnip and carrot pieces along with the crushed red pepper, coriander and stock. Bring the stock to a boil, cover the skillet and cook the vegetables until they are just tender — about five minutes.

Add the zucchini to the vegetables in the skillet. Cover the skillet again and cook the vegetables until the zucchini is barely tender — about three minutes. Add the red pepper pieces and the green scallion tops. Cook, uncovered, for three minutes.

With a fork, fluff up the couscous and transfer it to a large bowl. Pour the vegetables and cooking liquid over the pasta, mix, and serve at once.

Terrine of Butternut Squash and Egg Noodles

Serves 12 as a side dish
Working time: about 40 minutes
Total time: about 1 hour and 15 minutes

Calories **191**
Protein **6g.**
Cholesterol **47mg.**
Total fat **5g.**
Saturated fat **2g.**
Sodium **201mg.**

10 oz. wide egg noodles
¾ tsp. salt
½ tsp. ground cinnamon
½ tsp. ground coriander
1 tsp. ground allspice
freshly ground black pepper
1 large butternut squash (about 2½ lb.), peeled, halved lengthwise and seeded, the neck cut lengthwise into ¼-inch-thick slices, the rest cut into ¼-inch-thick crescents
2 tbsp. safflower oil
1 onion, finely chopped
1 egg and 3 egg whites, lightly beaten
1 tbsp. unsalted butter

Preheat the oven to 350° F. Combine the salt, spices and some pepper in a small bowl. Brush the squash pieces with 1 tablespoon of the oil and arrange them in a single layer on a baking sheet. Sprinkle the squash with half of the spice mixture and bake until softened — about 15 minutes. Leave the oven on.

While the squash cooks, bring 2 quarts of water with 1 teaspoon of salt to a boil. Pour the remaining tablespoon of oil into a skillet over medium heat. Add the onion and some more pepper and cook, stirring frequently, until the onion is translucent — about seven minutes. Meanwhile, add the noodles to the boiling water and cook them until they are almost *al dente* — about seven minutes.

Drain the noodles and return them to their pot. Add the egg and egg whites to the noodles along with the remaining spice mixture. Add the butter, ¼ cup of water and the onion, and stir until the butter is melted.

Butter a 9-by-5-inch loaf pan. Line the bottom and sides of the pan with squash slices, covering all surfaces completely; reserve about one third of the slices for the top. Add the noodle mixture and press it down to make it compact. Arrange the reserved squash slices evenly over the top and cover them with a piece of wax paper. Put a heavy, flat-bottomed object, such as a brick or an ovenproof skillet, on top of the wax paper to weight the contents down, then bake the terrine for 35 minutes. Let the terrine stand for 10 minutes before unmolding it.

To unmold the terrine, loosen it by running a knife around the inside of the pan, pressing it against the pan. Invert a serving dish over the pan, then turn both dish and pan over together. Carefully lift away the pan. Present the terrine whole or cut into serving slices; it is also good chilled.

Couscous with Fresh and Smoked Salmon, Yogurt and Dill

Serves 6
Working time: about 20 minutes
Total time: about 1 hour

Calories **187**
Protein **14g.**
Cholesterol **28mg.**
Total fat **6g.**
Saturated fat **2g.**
Sodium **161mg.**

1 cup couscous
8 oz. fresh salmon fillet, thinly sliced
1 oz. smoked salmon, julienned
juice of 1 lime
freshly ground black pepper
8 oz. plain low-fat yogurt
3 tbsp. finely cut fresh dill
⅛ tsp. salt

Arrange the fresh salmon slices in a single layer on a round, flat, ovenproof dish about 10 inches in diameter. Distribute the smoked salmon over the fresh salmon slices. Pour the lime juice over the fish and season it with a generous grinding of pepper. Let the salmon marinate at room temperature for at least 30 minutes.

To prepare the couscous, put it in a bowl and pour 1 cup of boiling water over it. Cover the bowl and let the couscous stand for at least five minutes.

Meanwhile, to cook the salmon, pour enough water into a saucepan approximately 8 inches in diameter to fill it about one third full. Bring the water to a rolling boil. Cover the dish containing the salmon tightly with aluminum foil, then set the dish atop the saucepan like a lid. Cook the fish over the boiling water until the fresh salmon is no longer translucent — about five minutes. Turn off the heat, but leave the assembly in place over the hot water so that the salmon stays warm until serving time.

Fluff the couscous with a fork, then stir in the yogurt, 2 tablespoons of the dill and the salt. Mound the mixture on a serving platter and arrange the salmon on top. Pour the marinade over the fish. Sprinkle the salmon with the remaining tablespoon of dill and serve immediately.

Afghan Noodles

Serves 6
Working time: about 35 minutes
Total time: about 45 minutes

Calories **350**
Protein **24g.**
Cholesterol **47mg.**
Total fat **12g.**
Saturated fat **5g.**
Sodium **326mg.**

8 oz. wide curly egg noodles
1 cup low-fat yogurt, drained in a fine-meshed sieve or a cheesecloth-lined sieve for 30 minutes
4 tbsp. chopped fresh mint, or 2 tbsp. dried mint
2½ tsp. chili powder
1 tbsp. fresh lemon juice
1 tbsp. safflower oil
1 onion, finely chopped
1 lb. lean ground beef
½ tsp. salt
1 ripe tomato, peeled, seeded and chopped
1 tbsp. unsalted butter

To prepare the sauce, combine the drained yogurt with 3 tablespoons of the fresh mint or 1½ tablespoons of the dried mint, ½ teaspoon of the chili powder and the lemon juice.

Heat the oil in a large, heavy-bottomed skillet over medium-high heat. Add the onion and sauté it for three minutes. Add the beef, the remaining 2 teaspoons of chili powder and the salt, and cook the mixture for six minutes, stirring frequently. Stir in the tomato and cook for two minutes more.

Meanwhile, cook the egg noodles in 3 quarts of boiling water with 1½ teaspoons of salt until they are *al dente* — about nine minutes. Drain the noodles and return them to the pot. Add the butter and stir gently until it melts and the noodles are coated.

To serve, transfer the hot noodles to a warmed serving platter. Pour the sauce over the noodles in a ring an inch or two in from the edge of the noodles, then arrange the beef mixture in the center of the ring. Sprinkle the remaining mint over the top of the assembly and serve immediately.

Egg Noodles with Poppy Seeds, Yogurt and Mushrooms

Serves 8 as a side dish
Working (and total) time: about 25 minutes

Calories **193**
Protein **6g.**
Cholesterol **28mg.**
Total fat **6g.**
Saturated fat **2g.**
Sodium **143mg.**

8 oz. medium egg noodles
¼ cup sour cream
½ cup low-fat yogurt
1 tbsp. poppy seeds
⅛ to ¼ tsp. cayenne pepper
2 tbsp. virgin olive oil
½ lb. mushrooms, wiped clean and thinly sliced (about 3 cups)
1 onion, chopped
¼ tsp. salt
½ cup dry white wine

In a small bowl, combine the sour cream, yogurt, poppy seeds, cayenne pepper and 1 tablespoon of the oil.

In a large, covered pot, cook the egg noodles in 3 quarts of boiling water with 1½ teaspoons of salt until they are *al dente* — about nine minutes.

While the noodles are cooking, heat the remaining tablespoon of oil in a large, heavy-bottomed skillet over medium-high heat. Add the mushrooms and onion, and sprinkle them with the ¼ teaspoon of salt. Cook, stirring frequently, until the mushrooms and onion are browned all over — five to seven minutes. Add the wine to the skillet and continue cooking, stirring, until almost all of the liquid has been absorbed — about three minutes more.

When the noodles are done, drain them and add them to the skillet. Add the yogurt-and-poppy-seed mixture, toss well and serve.

Noodles with Asparagus, Mushrooms and Prosciutto

Serves 4
Working (and total) time: about 20 minutes

Calories **443**	8 oz. wide egg noodles
Protein **17g.**	½ lb. asparagus, trimmed and peeled
Cholesterol **64mg.**	3 tbsp. virgin olive oil
Total fat **17g.**	1 onion, finely chopped
Saturated fat **5g.**	2 oz. shiitake mushrooms, sliced (about 1 cup), or 4 oz. button mushrooms
Sodium **348mg.**	2 garlic cloves, finely chopped
	freshly ground black pepper
	1½ oz. prosciutto, cut into strips ¼ inch wide and 1 inch long
	1 tsp. fresh lemon juice
	15 fresh basil leaves
	½ cup freshly grated Parmesan cheese

Cut each asparagus stalk diagonally into three pieces, then halve each piece lengthwise. Set the pieces aside.

Heat 1 tablespoon of the olive oil in a large, heavy-bottomed skillet over medium-high heat. Sauté the onion until it becomes translucent — about five minutes. Stir in the mushrooms, garlic and some pepper, and cook the mixture until the mushrooms are tender — about five minutes more. If you are using button mushrooms, cook them an additional four or five minutes to evaporate some of their moisture. Add the asparagus pieces and cook them until they are tender — another four to five minutes. Stir in the prosciutto, lemon juice and basil leaves.

While the mushrooms are cooking, add the noodles to 3 quarts of unsalted boiling water and cook them until they are *al dente* — approximately nine minutes. Drain the noodles and add them immediately to the skillet. Add the Parmesan cheese and the remaining 2 tablespoons of olive oil, and toss thoroughly. Serve at once on warmed plates.

3 *Rice and wheat noodles spill from drawers of Japanese chests in an Eastern setting that includes pungent ingredients associated with Asian pasta dishes.*

The World of Asian Noodles

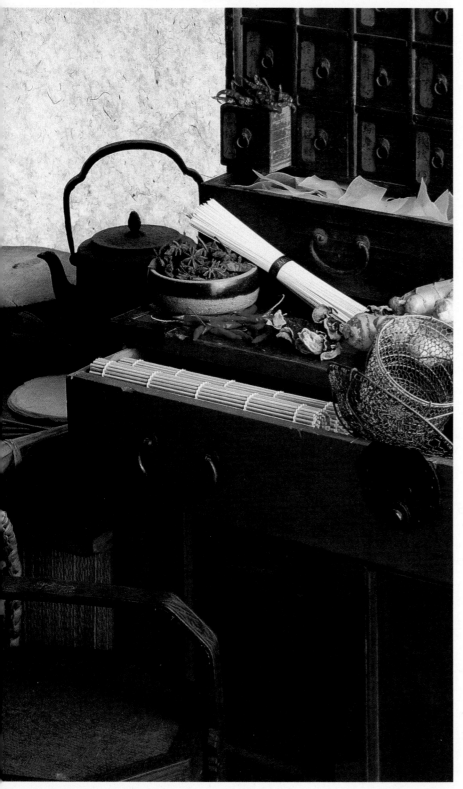

Only recently have many cooks made the happy discovery that there is a great deal more to pasta than the Italian kinds most people are familiar with — indeed, that there is a whole new world of pasta for them to explore. This is the world of Asian noodles and of the thin pasta wrappers that are used to cover egg rolls, spring rolls and other morsels. The noodles take so many forms — and are of such major importance to cuisines as varied as the Japanese, Chinese, Thai and Indonesian — that it is a wonder they could have been overlooked for so long. Not only can they be bought in the Asian markets that have proliferated around the country, but many are now available in supermarkets. Several can be made easily at home.

Fresh or dried, Asian noodles form the foundation of the 20 recipes to be found in this section. The noodles are in no way mysterious. Produced from wheat flour, rice flour or vegetable starch, they come mostly in strings or strands, some curled into neat round or oval skeins. Whatever form they take, all entice by their toothsomeness and taste. Because both rice noodles and vegetable-starch noodles are precooked as part of their manufacturing process, they need only be soaked in hot water to rehydrate them; occasionally they are boiled or simmered afterward.

Fresh egg noodles and dried wheat pastas are cooked the same way as Western pastas — in lots of boiling water. They too should be tested regularly for doneness and served *al dente*. When fresh Asian egg noodles are not available, substitute a dried Asian wheat noodle, or even a dried Western pasta such as vermicelli, spaghetti or linguine.

Techniques for finishing, serving and garnishing Asian noodles are described in this section as well. Among them are stratagems for re-creating the exciting flavors of Eastern dishes without incorporating the monosodium glutamate and excessive salt customarily associated with Asian food. Such tactics include reducing stocks and mushroom-soaking liquids, or building a flavor base from an infusion of such aromatics as ginger, garlic and lemon grass. In many of the dishes, a number of different ingredients are used in sparing amounts to create a bouquet of flavors — a practice common to both the new American cooking and traditional Asian cuisines. The recipes in this section thus tend to be longer than many appearing elsewhere in the book, and they are often more complex as well. But the reward will be dishes so complete in their satisfaction as to constitute meals in themselves.

A Panoply of Asian Pastas

WHEAT NOODLES

very thin wheat noodles
(somen)

flat wheat noodles

wonton wrappers

gyoza wrappers

nested wheat noodles

thin wheat noodles

fresh egg noodles

RICE NOODLES
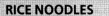

MUNG BEAN NOODLES
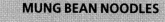

rice-paper wrappers

beanthread noodles
cellophane noodles

flat beanthread noodles

rice-noodle squares

All the Asian pastas called for by the recipes in this section are shown here. They have been divided into three basic categories and are identified generically; where appropriate, the Asian name most often associated with a pasta is also given. Since Asian pastas are likely to be sold under different names in a variety of languages, the cook would be well advised to learn what the three basic types look like and be guided by appearances when shopping for specific kinds.

rice vermicelli
rice sticks (mifen)

flat rice noodles

Pancit Guisado

THIS RECIPE IS ADAPTED FROM A CLASSIC PHILIPPINE NOODLE DISH
RESEMBLING PAELLA. NAM PRIK IS A THAI CHILI PASTE, AVAILABLE
IN SEVERAL VARIETIES IN SMALL JARS AT ASIAN MARKETS.

Serves 6
Working (and total) time: about 1 hour

Calories **329**
Protein **31g.**
Cholesterol **79mg.**
Total fat **13g.**
Saturated fat **3g.**
Sodium **538mg.**

12 oz. fresh Asian egg noodles, or 8 oz. dried vermicelli
2 tsp. nam prik
2 tbsp. rice wine or dry sherry
3 tbsp. low-sodium soy sauce
12 garlic cloves, 2 finely chopped and 10 thinly sliced
1 tsp. freshly grated lemon zest
6 oz. pork tenderloin, trimmed of all fat and cut into strips about 1 inch long and ½ inch wide
one 6-oz. chicken breast half, skinned, boned and cut into strips about 1 inch long and ½ inch wide
8 oz. small shrimp, peeled, the tail section of the shell left intact
2 slices low-salt bacon, cut into thin strips
2 medium onions, thinly sliced (about 2½ cups)
8 dried shiitake or Chinese black mushrooms, soaked in very hot water for 20 minutes, drained and squeezed dry, the soaking liquid reserved
1 cup unsalted chicken stock, reduced to ¼ cup
1 tbsp. Chinese black vinegar or balsamic vinegar

1 tbsp. finely chopped fresh oregano
2 tbsp. finely chopped cilantro
1 tbsp. fresh lemon juice
3 tbsp. safflower oil
1 tsp. finely chopped fresh ginger
2 small zucchini, sliced diagonally into thin ovals (about 1½ cups)
1 red bell pepper, seeded, deribbed and sliced lengthwise into thin strips, each strip sliced in half diagonally at the center
2 cups fresh bean sprouts, rinsed and drained
4 scallions, trimmed and chopped (about ½ cup)

In a large bowl, mix the nam prik with the wine, 1 tablespoon of the soy sauce, the finely chopped garlic and the lemon zest. Stir in the pork, chicken and shrimp. Cover the bowl and allow the mixture to marinate at room temperature for at least 30 minutes.

In a wok or a heavy-bottomed skillet, cook the bacon over medium-low heat until it renders some of its fat — about three minutes. Add the thinly sliced garlic and sauté it with the bacon, watching that the mixture does not burn, until the garlic turns faintly golden — about four minutes. Add the onions and cook them, stirring occasionally, until they are golden and very limp — about 20 minutes.

While the onions are cooking, put 4 quarts of water

on to boil. Slice the mushrooms into thin strips. Reduce the reserved mushroom-soaking liquid over medium-high heat to about ¼ cup. Add the noodles to the boiling water. Start testing them after three minutes and cook them until they are *al dente*. Drain the noodles and keep them warm.

In a large saucepan, combine the mushrooms, reduced mushroom liquid, reduced stock, vinegar, oregano, cilantro, the remaining 2 tablespoons of soy sauce and the lemon juice. Stir in the bacon-onion mixture and set the pan over very low heat to keep it warm.

Heat 1 tablespoon of the oil in a wok. Add the ginger and zucchini, and stir fry them for one minute. Add the red pepper and bean sprouts, and stir fry for one minute more. Toss the stir-fried vegetables with the bacon-onion mixture, then combine them with the noodles and transfer the mixture to a heated platter.

Wipe out the wok and pour in the remaining 2 tablespoons of oil. When the oil is very hot, add the pork, chicken and shrimp, and stir fry them for 90 seconds. Add the scallions and stir fry for 30 seconds more. Stir the meat and shrimp into the noodles and serve the dish immediately.

EDITOR'S NOTE: *This dish is equally tasty at room temperature. It may be prepared up to two hours beforehand and presented as part of a buffet. If you like, garnish it with lemon wedges, halved cherry tomatoes and oregano sprigs, and serve a fresh fruit salad with it.*

Eight-Treasure Noodles with Chinese Sausage

Serves 6
Working (and total) time: about 45 minutes

Calories **332**
Protein **20g.**
Cholesterol **13mg.**
Total fat **13g.**
Saturated fat **4g.**
Sodium **442mg.**

8 oz. dried flat wheat noodles or fettuccine
4 cups unsalted chicken stock
1½ tbsp. safflower oil
1 tbsp. grated fresh ginger
1 small red onion, cut into ¾-inch squares (about 1 cup)
1 red bell pepper, seeded, deribbed and cut into ¾-inch squares (about 1 cup)
3 lop cheong sausages, thinly sliced diagonally, simmered for 5 minutes in water to cover and drained, or 4 oz. barbecue pork (see editor's note, page 125), cut into ⅛-inch-thick slices
1½ cups snow peas, trimmed and halved diagonally
8 dried shiitake or Chinese black mushrooms, soaked in very hot water for 20 minutes, drained, stemmed and quartered
15 oz. canned baby corn, drained and rinsed
15 oz. canned straw mushrooms, drained
1½ cups broccoli florets, blanched in boiling water for 1 minute, refreshed under cold water and drained
1½ cups cauliflower florets, blanched in boiling water for 1 minute, refreshed under cold water and drained
2 tsp. cornstarch, mixed with 2 tbsp. water
1 tbsp. low-sodium soy sauce
1 tbsp. rice vinegar
1 tsp. dark sesame oil

Reduce the stock to about 1 cup and keep it hot.

Add the noodles to 4 quarts of boiling water with 2 teaspoons of salt; start testing them after three minutes and cook them until they are *al dente*. Drain the noodles and rinse them with cold water.

In a hot wok, heat the oil over medium-high heat. When the oil is hot but not smoking, add the ginger and onion, and stir fry them for 30 seconds. Put in the red pepper, sausage, snow peas, shiitake or Chinese black mushrooms and baby corn, and continue stir frying for one minute. Add the straw mushrooms, broccoli and cauliflower, and stir fry until all ingredients are very hot — about one minute more.

Stir the cornstarch mixture, soy sauce and vinegar into the hot stock. Pour this sauce into the wok and stir until it thickens, adding the sesame oil at the last minute. Put the noodles in the wok, toss them with the vegetables to heat them through, and then serve the dish immediately.

Imperial Garden Rolls

Serves 6 (18 rolls)
Working (and total) time: about 2 hours

Calories **274**
Protein **18g.**
Cholesterol **57mg.**
Total fat **1g.**
Saturated fat **0g.**
Sodium **555mg.**

18 rice-paper wrappers, about 6 inches in diameter
12 oz. lump crab meat, all bits of shell removed and discarded
2 tbsp. fresh lime juice
zest of 1 lime
½ jalapeño pepper (caution, page 33), seeded and very finely chopped (about 1 tsp.), or ¾ tsp. sambal oelek
1 tbsp. very finely chopped fresh mint
1 tbsp. very finely chopped cilantro
6 scallions, trimmed and very finely chopped (about ½ cup)
2 oz. beanthread noodles, covered with boiling water and soaked for 20 minutes, drained and cut into 2-inch lengths
2 cups snow peas, trimmed and thinly sliced lengthwise (about ½ lb.)
18 Nappa cabbage or celery cabbage leaves, the top 4 inches only
2 cups fresh bean sprouts, rinsed
1 red bell pepper, seeded, deribbed and julienned (about 36 strips)
3 red chili peppers (optional), soaked in warm water for 20 minutes if dried, each seeded and cut into 6 rounds (caution, page 33)
18 long scallion leaves for tying the packets
18 mint sprigs for garnish
18 cilantro sprigs for garnish
lime wedges for garnish (optional)
Sweet chili dipping sauce
1 garlic clove, chopped
2 tsp. sweet chili sauce
2 tbsp. fresh lime juice, including as much pulp as can be scraped out with a spoon
2 tbsp. low-sodium soy sauce

For the dipping sauce, combine the garlic, sweet chili sauce, lime juice, soy sauce and 4 tablespoons of water in a small serving bowl.

To prepare the filling, combine the crab meat with the lime juice, lime zest, jalapeño pepper or sambal oelek, chopped mint, chopped cilantro, chopped scallions and the beanthread noodles. Refrigerate the filling for 30 minutes to allow the flavors to blend.

Meanwhile, blanch the snow-pea strips in 2 quarts of boiling water for 20 seconds and remove them with a slotted spoon. Use the same water to blanch the cabbage leaves and bean sprouts in separate batches for 20 seconds each. Refresh the blanched vegetables in cold water, drain them and keep them separate. Toss the bean sprouts with the crab-meat filling.

Arrange all the ingredients on a work surface. Set out two large plates, one of them filled about ¼ inch deep with warm water.

To make a roll, immerse a sheet of rice paper in the warm water for 30 seconds and transfer it to the empty plate. Allow the paper to rest until it is uniformly soft. Arrange two bell-pepper strips and a few snow-pea strips on the upper half of the circle so that their tips ▶

overhang the edge. Mound about ¼ cup of the crab-meat mixture atop the vegetables and carefully fold the bottom third of the sheet up over the filling. Fold in one side of the sheet, place a chili-pepper round on the fold, then fold in the second side. Secure the roll by tying a scallion leaf around it. Repeat the process with the remaining wrappers, vegetables and filling.

To serve as a main course, carefully place each roll on a cabbage leaf. Arrange three packets in the pattern of a fan on each of six plates and garnish them with the mint and cilantro sprigs and the lime wedges, if desired. Dip the rolls in the sauce as you eat them.

EDITOR'S NOTE: *This recipe yields 18 individual servings for appetizers or a first course, or six main-course servings consisting of three rolls each. When serving the packets as a first course, accompany them with grilled fish. If the rolls are prepared in advance, keep them moist by misting them with water from a spray bottle.*

When buying rice papers, inspect them to ensure that only a few, if any, are cracked or flaked. Because the papers break easily when dry and may tear when moistened, they should be handled with care at all times. Store any unused papers in tightly sealed plastic bags at room temperature.

enough water to cover them. Bring the water to a boil, then reduce the heat to low and poach the breasts until they are tender — about 10 minutes. Remove the chicken with a slotted spoon; discard the cooking liquid. As soon as the chicken is cool enough to handle, separate the meat from the bones. Discard the skin and bones and shred the meat by hand. Cover the chicken and set it aside in a warm place.

Add the noodles to 4 quarts of boiling water with 2 teaspoons of salt. Start testing the noodles after three minutes and cook them until they are *al dente*. Drain the noodles, then rinse them with cold water and set them aside in a colander.

In a hot wok or a heavy-bottomed skillet, heat 1 tablespoon of the safflower oil over medium-high heat. Add the broccoli florets and stir fry them until they turn bright green. Add 1 tablespoon of the sherry along with the sugar, and stir fry for 30 seconds more. Transfer the broccoli to a bowl, toss it with the sesame seeds and cover the bowl to keep the broccoli warm.

Heat the remaining 2 tablespoons of safflower oil in the wok or skillet until the oil is hot but not smoking. Add the chopped peppers and stir fry them for 30 seconds. Pour in the soy sauce and the remaining ½ tablespoon of sherry, then add the chicken and the scallions, and stir fry the mixture for one minute more.

Pour boiling water over the noodles in the colander to reheat them. Divide the noodles among four serving bowls and ladle the simmering stock over them in equal amounts. Divide the broccoli and the chicken-scallion mixture into four parts. In each bowl, arrange the chicken on one side and the broccoli on the other in a yin-yang pattern. Serve immediately.

Chicken, Broccoli and Chilies on Egg Noodles

Serves 4
Working (and total) time: about 35 minutes

Calories **303**	
Protein **28g.**	12 oz. fresh Asian egg noodles, or 8 oz. dried vermicelli or thin spaghetti
Cholesterol **28mg.**	2 cups unsalted chicken stock
Total fat **14g.**	3½ tbsp. rice wine or dry sherry
Saturated fat **2g.**	1 tsp. dark sesame oil
Sodium **455mg.**	¼ tsp. salt
	white pepper
	2 chicken breast halves
	3 tbsp. safflower oil
	5 oz. broccoli florets (about 2 cups)
	¼ tsp. sugar
	½ tsp. sesame seeds
	2 jalapeño peppers, seeded and very finely chopped (caution, page 33)
	1 tbsp. low-sodium soy sauce
	4 scallions, trimmed and finely chopped

Bring the stock to a boil in a saucepan. Add 2 tablespoons of the wine, the sesame oil, the salt and some pepper, and return the liquid to a boil. Reduce the heat to low and let the stock simmer very slowly.

Put the chicken breast halves in a pot and pour in

Nest of the Phoenix

THE CONCENTRIC RINGS OF VEGETABLES AND NOODLES
IN THIS SALAD SUGGEST THE RISING SUN, OFTEN SYMBOLIZED
BY THE PHOENIX.

Serves 8
Working (and total) time: about 1 hour and 15 minutes

Calories **353**
Protein **19g.**
Cholesterol **77mg.**
Total fat **5g.**
Saturated fat **1g.**
Sodium **293mg.**

1 lb. flat rice noodles
1¼ lb. small cooked shrimp
½ cup fresh lime juice
grated zest of 1 lime (about 1 tsp.)
3 tsp. sweet chili sauce
4 tbsp. chopped fresh mint
1 tbsp. chopped cilantro
2 cups snow peas, stems and strings removed, blanched in boiling water for 1 minute, drained and julienned
2 tsp. low-sodium soy sauce
½ tsp. dark sesame oil
1 tbsp. chopped fresh basil
1½ tbsp. safflower oil
2 tsp. finely chopped fresh ginger

3 large carrots, peeled and julienned (about 2½ cups)
6 tbsp. fresh lemon juice
5 scallions, sliced diagonally into very thin ovals (about ½ cup)
3 cups fresh bean sprouts, rinsed and drained
3 tbsp. unsweetened coconut milk
½ tsp. salt
1½ tsp. finely chopped fresh citrus leaf, center vein removed, or 1½ tsp. grated lime zest

Garnish

1 head Boston lettuce
1 large red bell pepper, seeded, deribbed and halved lengthwise, each half sliced crosswise into thin strips
mint sprigs
2 lemons (optional), each cut into 8 wedges

In a large bowl, combine the shrimp, 2 tablespoons of the lime juice, the lime zest, 1 teaspoon of the sweet chili sauce, 1 tablespoon of the chopped mint, and the cilantro. Set the bowl aside.

In another bowl, combine the snow peas with the ▶

soy sauce, sesame oil and basil. Set that bowl aside too.

Pour enough boiling water over the noodles to cover them, and let them soak for 15 minutes. Drain the noodles and rinse them in cold water; drain them thoroughly and set them aside.

While the noodles are soaking, pour ½ tablespoon of the safflower oil into a heated wok or a heavy-bottomed skillet over high heat. When the oil is hot, add the ginger and the carrots. Reduce the heat to medium and stir fry the carrots for one minute. Add 2 tablespoons of water, cover the wok, and steam the contents for two minutes. Transfer the carrots to a bowl and toss them with 2 tablespoons of the lemon juice. Set the bowl aside.

Wipe out the wok and heat the remaining tablespoon of safflower oil in it. Add the scallions and stir fry them for 30 seconds, then add the bean sprouts and stir fry them for one minute more. Spread the scallions and sprouts on a plate so they may cool.

Prepare the dressing for the noodles: In a large bowl, combine the coconut milk, salt, and citrus leaf or zest with the remaining 6 tablespoons of lime juice, the remaining 2 teaspoons of sweet chili sauce, the remaining 3 tablespoons of chopped mint and the remaining 4 tablespoons of lemon juice. Toss the dressing with the drained noodles and set them aside.

To assemble the nest of the phoenix, line a very large platter with the lettuce leaves. Fill the dish with the noodles, making a wide, shallow well in their center. Tuck the red-pepper strips between the lettuce leaves and the noodles all the way around the dish.

Arrange the carrots in a ring about 2 inches in from the edge of the noodles. Next make a smaller circle of the snow peas just inside the carrot ring, then a ring of the scallion-and-sprout mixture just inside the snow peas. Mound the shrimp in the center and garnish the phoenix nest with the mint sprigs and the lemon wedges if you are using them. Serve immediately, at room temperature.

EDITOR'S NOTE: *If canned or frozen unsweetened coconut milk is unavailable, the coconut milk may be made at home: Mix 3 tablespoons of unsweetened dried coconut in a blender with 3 tablespoons of very hot water and strain the mixture.*

Pork-Filled Dumplings

Serves 8 as an appetizer
Working time: about 50 minutes
Total time: about 1 hour

Calories **78**
Protein **8g.**
Cholesterol **8mg.**
Total fat **2g.**
Saturated fat **1g.**
Sodium **255mg.**

32 wonton wrappers
4 oz. boneless pork loin, trimmed of all fat and finely chopped
¼ cup water chestnuts, chopped
¼ cup bamboo shoots, rinsed, drained and chopped
1 tbsp. low-sodium soy sauce
2 tbsp. dry sherry
1 scallion, finely chopped
1 tsp. finely chopped fresh ginger
2 dried shiitake or Chinese black mushrooms, soaked in very hot water for 20 minutes, drained, stemmed, squeezed dry and chopped
1 cup unsalted chicken stock, mixed with 1 cup water
1 tsp. sweet chili sauce
1 tbsp. Chinese black vinegar or balsamic vinegar
1 tbsp. bean paste

To prepare the filling, combine the pork with the water chestnuts, bamboo shoots, soy sauce, sherry, scallion, ginger and mushrooms in a large bowl.

Place 1 teaspoon of the filling in the center of a wonton wrapper. Moisten two adjacent edges of the wrapper and fold it into the shape of a wonton *(technique, page 123)*. Repeat the process with the remaining wonton wrappers and filling.

Pour the stock into a skillet large enough to hold the wontons in a single layer and bring the stock to a boil. (If your skillet is not big enough, cook the wontons in batches.) Gently lower the dumplings into the stock, then reduce the heat until the liquid is at a full simmer. Cover the skillet and cook the wontons until their wrappers are tender — about seven minutes. With a slotted spoon, transfer the dumplings to heated plates.

Stir the chili sauce, vinegar and bean paste into the stock remaining in the skillet. Pour some of this sauce over the dumplings and serve the rest separately.

EDITOR'S NOTE: *If you are using fresh water chestnuts, they should be peeled and trimmed of their dark spots before they are chopped and added to the filling.*

Warm Sichuan Noodles with Spiced Beef

Serves 6
Working time: about 30 minutes
Total time: about 1 hour

Calories **281**	1 lb. fresh Asian egg noodles, or 12 oz. dried vermicelli
Protein **29g.**	¾ lb. beef tenderloin or lean sirloin, trimmed of all fat
Cholesterol **28mg.**	
Total fat **12g.**	8 dried shiitake or Chinese black mushrooms, soaked in
Saturated fat **2g.**	very hot water for 20 minutes and drained
Sodium **340mg.**	4 scallions, thinly sliced diagonally
	1½ tbsp. safflower oil

Sesame-soy marinade

¼ cup low-sodium soy sauce
2 tbsp. Chinese black vinegar or balsamic vinegar
2 tbsp. rice vinegar
1 to 2 tsp. chili paste with garlic
½ tsp. very finely chopped garlic
1½ tsp. very finely chopped fresh ginger
1 tsp. sugar
1 tsp. dark sesame oil
2 tbsp. safflower oil
2 tbsp. toasted sesame seeds, crushed with a mortar and pestle
5 scallions, very finely chopped (about ¾ cup)
½ cup cilantro, coarsely chopped

Garnish

1 small cucumber, scored lengthwise with a fork and thinly sliced
1 tbsp. toasted sesame seeds
cilantro sprigs

Combine the marinade ingredients in a bowl and set the marinade aside.

Cut the beef across the grain into julienne about 1½ inches long and ⅛ inch thick. Cut off and discard the mushroom stems, and slice the caps into strips about ⅛ inch wide. In a bowl, combine the beef, mush-rooms and scallions with one third of the marinade. Let the beef marinate for 30 minutes.

At the end of the marinating time, put 4 quarts of water on to boil. Drain and discard any excess marinade from the beef mixture. Heat the 1½ tablespoons of safflower oil in a heavy-bottomed skillet or a wok; add the mushrooms, scallions and beef strips, and sauté them for one minute. Set the beef mixture aside on a large plate, spreading it out so that it cools rapidly.

Add the noodles to the boiling water. Start testing them after three minutes and cook them until they are *al dente*. Drain the noodles and transfer them to a large bowl. Add the remaining two thirds of the marinade and toss it with the noodles.

To serve, arrange the cucumber slices in an overlapping pattern around the edge of a large plate. Arrange the noodles in the center of the plate, partly covering the cucumbers. Make a shallow well in the center of the noodles and spoon the beef mixture into the well. Sprinkle the tablespoon of sesame seeds over all and garnish the top with a few fresh cilantro sprigs. Serve at room temperature.

EDITOR'S NOTE: *A colorful salad of fresh fruit, tossed with unsweetened coconut milk and fresh lemon juice, and garnished with mint, makes a delightful accompaniment.*

Shining Noodle Salad with Beef and Tomato

Serves 6
Working time: about 30 minutes
Total time: about 1 hour

Calories **267**
Protein **16g.**
Cholesterol **28mg.**
Total fat **6g.**
Saturated fat **2g.**
Sodium **339mg.**

8 oz. flat beanthread noodles or rice noodles
two 6-oz. beef tenderloin steaks, trimmed of all fat
½ cup thinly sliced red onion
grated zest of 1 lime
4 tbsp. fresh lime juice
2 tsp. finely chopped cilantro
2 tsp. very finely chopped fresh lemon grass, or 1½ tsp. grated lemon zest
2 tsp. finely chopped fresh mint
½ tsp. finely chopped hot chili pepper (caution, page 33), or ½ tsp. sambal oelek
½ tsp. finely chopped garlic
3 tbsp. low-sodium soy sauce
1 tbsp. safflower oil
½ tsp. sugar
2 small heads Boston lettuce
3 ripe tomatoes, thinly sliced
mint leaves for garnish

Broil the steaks until they are rare and allow them to cool. Cut each steak in half lengthwise. Thinly slice each half into pieces about ⅛-inch thick, and toss the pieces with the onion slices. Set the mixture aside.

In a large bowl, combine the lime zest and juice, cilantro, lemon grass or lemon zest, mint, chili pepper or sambal oelek, garlic, soy sauce, oil and sugar. Pour half of this marinade over the beef and onion slices, reserving the other half of the marinade for the noodles. Toss well, then cover the beef and let it marinate at room temperature for 30 minutes.

Pour enough boiling water over the noodles to cover them. Soak the noodles until they are *al dente* — 10 to 15 minutes, depending on their thickness. Drain the noodles, rinse them in cold water, and drain them ▶

once again. Wrap the noodles in a clean towel and squeeze out most of their moisture. Cut the noodles into 6-inch lengths and toss them with the reserved half of the marinade.

To serve, arrange some lettuce leaves on each of six plates. At one side of each plate, just inside the edge of the leaves, arrange several tomato slices in a crescent. Mound some noodles next to the tomatoes. Arrange the beef slices on top of the noodles, then distribute the onion strips around the beef in a flower pattern. Garnish the salads with the mint leaves and serve them at room temperature.

EDITOR'S NOTE: *To give the onion slices an intriguingly different shape, first halve an onion lengthwise, then cut one of the halves lengthwise into thin strips resembling crescents.*

Nonya Rice Noodles with Shrimp

A BLEND OF CHINESE AND MALAYSIAN INGREDIENTS, NONYA DISHES ARE DISTINCTIVELY RICH AND SPICY. NONYA COOKING DEVELOPED IN THE 19TH CENTURY WITH THE INFLUX OF CHINESE TIN MINERS INTO THE MALAY PENINSULA.

Serves 6
Working (and total) time: about 45 minutes

Calories **349**
Protein **15g.**
Cholesterol **62mg.**
Total fat **8g.**
Saturated fat **3g.**
Sodium **358mg.**

12 oz. flat rice noodles
¾ lb. small shrimp, shelled
2 tsp. very finely chopped fresh lemon grass, or 1½ tsp. freshly grated lemon zest
1 tsp. very finely chopped fresh ginger
½ tsp. very finely chopped garlic
½ tsp. salt
2 tbsp. safflower oil
½ cup unsweetened coconut milk
1½ cups unsalted chicken stock, reduced to 1 cup
6 tbsp. fresh lemon juice
2 tsp. low-sodium soy sauce
2 tsp. sweet chili sauce
2 tsp. ground coriander
1 large onion, halved lengthwise and thinly sliced
1 red bell pepper, seeded, deribbed and thinly sliced
1 lemon, cut into wedges (optional)
1 bunch watercress (optional)

Pour enough boiling water over the rice noodles to cover them, and let them soak for 15 minutes. In a large bowl, combine the shrimp with the lemon grass, ginger, garlic and salt. (If you are using lemon zest in place of the lemon grass, set it aside for later use.)

Heat 1 tablespoon of the oil in a hot wok or a heavy-bottomed skillet over high heat. Add the shrimp mixture and stir fry it until the shrimp are barely cooked — about three minutes. Transfer the shrimp to a plate. Pour out and reserve any juices left in the wok, then wipe the wok clean.

In a saucepan, combine the coconut milk, stock, lemon juice, soy sauce and chili sauce. Bring the liquid just to a boil. Heat the remaining tablespoon of oil in the wok. Add the ground coriander and onion, and gently stir fry them until the onion is limp — about four minutes. Add the red pepper and stir fry the mixture for one minute more.

Drain the noodles and add them to the red pepper and onion in the wok. Pour in the coconut-milk mixture and the reserved juices from the shrimp. Cook over medium heat, stirring, until most of the liquid has evaporated. If you are using lemon zest in place of the lemon grass, add it now. Stir in the shrimp and briefly heat them through. Serve the dish immediately, garnished, if you like, with the lemon wedges and the watercress.

EDITOR'S NOTE: *If canned or frozen unsweetened coconut milk is unavailable, the coconut milk may be made at home: Mix ½ cup of unsweetened dried coconut in a blender with ½ cup of very hot water and strain the mixture.*

Burmese Curried Noodles with Scallops and Broccoli

Serves 6
Working (and total) time: about 35 minutes

Calories **278**
Protein **26g.**
Cholesterol **23mg.**
Total fat **9g.**
Saturated fat **1g.**
Sodium **440mg.**

12 oz. dried rice-noodle squares or other rice noodles
3 tbsp. safflower oil
1 large onion, chopped (about 2 cups)
3 tsp. finely chopped garlic
1 tbsp. finely chopped fresh ginger
1 tsp. ground turmeric
½ tsp. ground cumin
1 tbsp. ground coriander
12 oz. broccoli florets (from about 2 medium stalks)
grated zest of 1 orange (about 1½ tsp.)
¼ cup fresh orange juice
2 tbsp. fresh lemon juice
½ tsp. salt
12 oz. sea scallops, each sliced in half horizontally (about 1½ cups)
4 scallions, trimmed and finely chopped (about ½ cup)
8 oz. fresh water chestnuts, peeled and sliced, or 8 oz. canned sliced water chestnuts, rinsed and drained (about 1 cup)
⅓ cup thinly sliced shallots (optional), stir fried in ¼ cup safflower oil until evenly browned and crisp, drained on paper towels

Heat 1 tablespoon of the oil in a hot wok or a heavy-bottomed skillet over medium heat. Add the onion, 1 teaspoon of the garlic, the ginger, turmeric, cumin and coriander. Cook, adding water as needed to prevent scorching, until the onion is soft and browned — about 15 minutes.

Heat 1 tablespoon of the oil in a skillet over medium heat. Add 1 teaspoon of the garlic and cook it for 30 seconds, stirring. Add the broccoli, cover the skillet, and cook the mixture for three minutes. Uncover the skillet and continue cooking, stirring, until the broccoli is tender — about one minute more.

Meanwhile, discard any noodles that are stuck together. Cook the remaining noodles in 4 quarts of boiling water with 2 teaspoons of salt. Start testing them after five minutes and cook them until they are *al dente*. Drain the noodles, add them to the onion mixture, and toss gently. Add the orange zest, orange juice, lemon juice and salt, and toss thoroughly.

Heat the remaining tablespoon of oil in a wok or a skillet. Add the scallops, the remaining teaspoon of garlic, the scallions and the water chestnuts. Stir fry the scallops and vegetables until they are barely done — one to two minutes.

Arrange the noodles on a serving platter. Distribute the broccoli around them, then spoon the scallops onto the noodles. Garnish the dish with the stir-fried shallots if you are using them, and serve immediately.

Shrimp Pot Stickers

Serves 8 as an appetizer
Working (and total) time: about 1 hour and 30 minutes

Calories **207**
Protein **9g.**
Cholesterol **46mg.**
Total fat **8g.**
Saturated fat **1g.**
Sodium **259mg.**

1½ cups unbleached all-purpose flour
4 tbsp. safflower oil
Shrimp filling
¾ lb. shrimp, peeled and finely chopped
4 dried shiitake or Chinese black mushrooms, soaked in very hot water for 20 minutes, drained, stemmed and chopped
8 oz. fresh water chestnuts, peeled and finely chopped, or 8 oz. canned water chestnuts, rinsed, drained and finely chopped
4 scallions, trimmed and finely chopped
1 tbsp. finely chopped fresh ginger
2 tsp. finely chopped garlic
2 tsp. low-sodium soy sauce
1 tsp. dry sherry
½ tsp. dark sesame oil
⅛ tsp. Asian chili sauce or hot red-pepper sauce
Hot dipping sauce
2 tbsp. low-sodium soy sauce
2 tbsp. rice vinegar
½ tsp. dark sesame oil
½ tsp. sugar
2 tsp. finely chopped fresh ginger
1 tsp. finely chopped garlic
⅛ tsp. Asian chili sauce or hot red-pepper sauce
1 tsp. sliced scallions

To make the dumpling dough, first place ¾ cup of the flour in a mixing bowl. Slowly add ¼ cup of cold water, stirring with a fork until the flour can be gathered into a dry, crumbly ball. Set the dough aside.

Place the remaining ¾ cup of flour in another mixing bowl and slowly add ½ cup of boiling water, stirring it in with a fork. When all the hot water has been absorbed, gather the dough into a ball and turn it out onto a lightly floured surface. Knead the hot-water dough until it is smooth and soft — about two minutes.

Combine the hot-water dough with the cold-water dough; knead the two together to form one smooth, elastic dough — four to five minutes. Then cover it with an inverted bowl and let it rest for 30 minutes.

To prepare the filling, put the shrimp in a large mixing bowl with the remaining filling ingredients. Stir the contents of the bowl thoroughly. Cover the bowl with plastic wrap and refrigerate the filling until you have prepared the dumpling wrappers.

In a separate bowl, stir together the dipping-sauce ingredients. Set the sauce aside.

To prepare the dough rounds by hand, first divide the rested dough in two. Shape the two pieces into ropelike strands 1½ inches in diameter by rolling them back and forth on a lightly floured surface. Slice each rope crosswise into ¾-inch-thick rounds. Dip the two ends of each round in flour.

Gently flatten one of the rounds in the palm of your ▶

Pleating Pot Stickers

1 *ROLLING OUT THE WRAPPER. On a lightly floured surface, flatten a dough round with a small rolling pin, rotating the piece to produce a 3½-inch circle. Roll out the other wrappers; stack them to prevent drying.*

2 *ADDING THE FILLING. Place the filling on a wrapper, slightly above the center. Moisten a fingertip and run it along the lower half of the wrapper's rim. Fold the lower half over the filling and pinch the top to close it.*

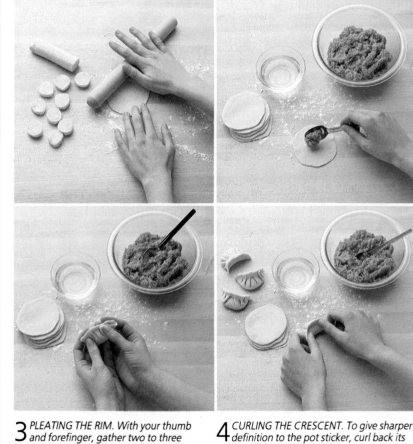

3 *PLEATING THE RIM. With your thumb and forefinger, gather two to three pleats on each side of the pot sticker, sealing the edge and allowing the filling to plump up. This creates a crescent shape.*

4 *CURLING THE CRESCENT. To give sharper definition to the pot sticker, curl back its ends and pinch them. Set it aside on a lightly floured surface and proceed to fill the remaining wrappers in the same way.*

hand. Put the round on a flour-dusted work surface and roll it out as demonstrated on page 117. Flatten and roll out the remaining rounds in the same way, keeping the finished circles and unformed rounds covered with a slightly damp cloth as you work.

As a simpler alternative to preparing the dough rounds by hand, divide the rested dough into quarters and roll out each piece with a pasta machine. Using a 3-inch-round cutter, cut the sheets of dough into circles. Keep them covered with a slightly damp cloth.

To make the dumplings, place 1½ tablespoons of the filling slightly off center on a circle. Fold the circle into a crescent-shaped dumpling as shown here. Repeat the process with the remaining circles, covering the dumplings with a slightly damp cloth as they are completed. (The dumplings can be made ahead of time and refrigerated on a lightly floured tray covered with plastic wrap.)

Cook the dumplings in two batches: Pour 2 tablespoons of the safflower oil into a large, heavy-bottomed skillet over high heat. Arrange half of the dumplings in the oil in a single layer without touching one another. Reduce the heat to medium and cook the dumplings until they turn golden brown on the bottom. Add enough cold water to come two thirds of the way up the sides of the dumplings. Cover the skillet partway and cook the dumplings until they have absorbed most of the liquid — eight to 10 minutes. Remove the dumplings with a slotted spoon and set them aside on paper towels to drain. Transfer the dumplings to a heated serving platter. Cook the second batch the same way in the remaining 2 tablespoons of safflower oil. Serve the dumplings with the dipping sauce.

EDITOR'S NOTE: *Gyoza wrappers, available in Asian markets, may be substituted for the fresh dough in this recipe.*

Lobster Noodles with Treasures of the Sea

Serves 6
Working time: about 45 minutes
Total time: about 1 hour

Calories **287**
Protein **33g.**
Cholesterol **71mg.**
Total fat **9g.**
Saturated fat **1g.**
Sodium **513mg.**

1 lb. fresh Asian egg noodles, or 12 oz. dried vermicelli
1 live lobster (about 2½ lb.)
5 oz. trimmed monkfish fillets, cut into 12 equal cubes
5 oz. sea scallops (12 small scallops, or 6 large ones, cut in half)
6 slender summer squash (3 yellow squash and 3 zucchini), scrubbed, each cut into 4 chunks, blanched in boiling water for 2 minutes and refreshed with cold water
Ginger-brandy marinade
2 tsp. very finely chopped garlic
2 tsp. very finely chopped fresh ginger
2 tsp. fermented black beans, rinsed and crushed
2 tbsp. brandy
¼ tsp. salt
1 tbsp. safflower oil
Garlic-scallion sauce
1 tbsp. safflower oil
1 tbsp. very finely chopped garlic
1 tsp. very finely chopped fresh ginger
5 scallions, trimmed and finely chopped (about ½ cup)
2 tsp. fermented black beans, rinsed and crushed
¼ tsp. sugar
1 tbsp. low-sodium soy sauce

Pour enough water into a 6-quart pot to fill it about 3 inches deep, and bring the water to a boil. Add the lobster, cover the pot, and cook for five minutes. Combine the marinade ingredients in a bowl and set aside.

Remove the lobster from the pot and set the lobster aside. Remove 1 cup of the lobster-cooking liquid and reserve it. Add enough water to the liquid remaining in the pot to make about 4 quarts; set it aside for cooking the noodles.

When the lobster is cool enough to handle, twist off the tail section and the claws. Working over a bowl to catch the juices, pull apart the body and remove the tomalley and the coral if there is any. Add them to the bowl and set aside. Cut the lobster tail in half lengthwise, then carefully remove the meat from the two halves (it will not be completely cooked); cut each half crosswise into six equal pieces. Add the tail meat, monkfish and scallops to the marinade, stir to coat the seafood, then let the mixture stand for 30 minutes. Remove the meat from the remaining pieces of lobster, dice it, and add it to the bowl containing the tomalley, coral and juice.

Preheat the broiler and bring the 4 quarts of lobster water to a boil. Thread the seafood and squash onto 12 skewers in the following order: monkfish, squash, lobster tail meat, squash, scallop. Six of the skewers should hold zucchini chunks; the other six should hold yellow squash. Reserve any extra marinade.

Add the noodles to the boiling lobster water. Start testing the noodles after three minutes and cook them until they are *al dente.*

While the noodles are cooking, make the sauce. Pour the tablepoon of oil into a hot wok. Add the garlic, ginger and scallions, and stir fry them for one minute over medium-high heat. Add the black beans, sugar and soy sauce along with the reserved lobster juice, tomalley, coral and diced lobster meat, the reserved cup of lobster-cooking liquid and any remaining marinade. Stir fry until the lobster is cooked — one to two minutes. Drain the noodles, add them to the wok, and toss them with the sauce.

Broil the skewers for about four minutes, turning them frequently to ensure even cooking.

To serve, arrange a portion of the noodles on each of six heated plates. Top each serving with two skewers and serve immediately.

Thai Chicken in Broth with Lemon Grass and Cellophane Noodles

Serves 4
Working time: about 30 minutes
Total time: about 1 hour

Calories **221**
Protein **18g.**
Cholesterol **38mg.**
Total fat **4g.**
Saturated fat **1g.**
Sodium **343mg.**

2 oz. beanthread (cellophane) noodles, tied together
1½ quarts unsalted chicken stock
2 chicken breast halves, skinned and boned (about 8 oz.)
½ cup cloud-ear mushrooms, soaked in very hot water for 20 minutes, then cut into thin strips
3 stalks fresh lemon grass, bruised with the flat of a knife and knotted, or 1½ tsp. grated lemon zest
2 citrus leaves, or 1 tbsp. fresh lime juice
4 thin slices fresh ginger
10 garlic cloves, peeled
2 tsp. fish sauce
2 tbsp. sweet chili sauce
cilantro leaves for garnish

Pour the stock into a heavy-bottomed ovenproof casserole and bring it to a boil. Add the beanthread noodles, the chicken breast halves, the cloud-ear strips, and the lemon grass and citrus leaves if you are using them. (If you are using lemon zest and lime juice in place of the lemon grass and citrus leaves, do not add them yet.) Thread the ginger slices and the garlic cloves onto skewers or wooden picks, and add them to the stock along with the fish sauce. Cover the casserole and remove it from the heat. Let the chicken stand undisturbed for 30 minutes.

Remove the chicken from the stock and set it aside to cool. Remove the lemon grass, ginger and garlic from the stock and discard them.

When the chicken is cool enough to handle, break it into shreds with your fingers. Remove the noodles from the stock, then untie them and cut them into 2-inch lengths. Reheat the stock; add the chicken, noodles and sweet chili sauce. If you are substituting lemon zest and lime juice, add them now. Ladle the mixture into individual bowls and garnish each serving with the cilantro leaves. Serve immediately.

Beijing Wheat Noodles with Braised Lamb and Scallions

Serves 4
Working time: about 40 minutes
Total time: about 2 hours

Calories **393**
Protein **23g.**
Cholesterol **33mg.**
Total fat **21g.**
Saturated fat **8g.**
Sodium **405mg.**

8 oz. fresh Asian wheat noodles (egg noodles), or 6 oz. dried vermicelli
2 bunches scallions
2 tbsp. safflower oil
8 oz. boned lamb shoulder, trimmed of all fat
4 large garlic cloves, sliced
1 cup unsalted lamb or beef stock
½ cup red wine
1 tbsp. low-sodium soy sauce
1 tsp. chili paste with garlic
8 oz. fresh water chestnuts, peeled and sliced, or 8 oz. canned sliced water chestnuts, drained and rinsed
1 star anise

Trim and chop one bunch of the scallions. Heat 1 tablespoon of the oil in a hot heavy-bottomed skillet over medium-high heat. Add the lamb and sear it until it is browned on all sides. Transfer the lamb to a heavy-bottomed 2-quart saucepan or casserole and set it aside. Add the garlic and chopped scallions to the skillet. Stir fry them over medium heat for three minutes,

adding a little water if necessary to prevent sticking.

Pour the stock into the skillet, scraping loose any bits that are stuck to the sides. Add this scallion-stock mixture to the lamb in the saucepan. Stir the wine, soy sauce, chili paste, water chestnuts and star anise into the lamb mixture. Bring the liquid to a boil, then reduce the heat to low, and cover the pan. Simmer the mixture, turning the lamb once, until the meat is tender — about one hour and 15 minutes.

When the lamb is finished cooking, put 4 quarts of water on to boil with 2 teaspoons of salt.

Remove the lamb, water chestnuts and star anise from the braising liquid; discard the star anise. Reserve the liquid. When the meat is cool enough to handle, shred it by hand. Slice the remaining scallions diagonally into thin ovals. Heat the remaining tablespoon of oil in a skillet over high heat. Add the scallion slices and stir fry them for one minute. Stir in the lamb and water chestnuts; stir fry for one minute more.

Add the noodles to the boiling water. Reheat the braising liquid. Start testing the noodles after three minutes and cook them until they are *al dente*. Drain the noodles, add them to the braising liquid, and toss them with the liquid; then arrange the noodles in a warmed serving dish and top them with the lamb mixture. Serve immediately.

EDITOR'S NOTE: *Star anise, sold in dried florets resembling stars, tastes much like anise seed. Ground star anise is a component of Chinese five-spice powder.*

Duckling Dumplings and Ginger-Plum Sauce

CLOUD-EAR MUSHROOMS ARE ALSO CALLED TREE EARS, WOOD EARS AND BLACK FUNGUS. THEY COME IN SMALL CHIPS THAT OPEN INTO PETALS WHEN SOAKED IN HOT WATER. CUT AWAY THE TOUGH INNER PORTION BEFORE CHOPPING THE MUSHROOMS.

Serves 6 (36 dumplings)
Working time: about 1 hour
Total time: about 1 hour and 30 minutes

Calories **193**
Protein **19g.**
Cholesterol **43mg.**
Total fat **3g.**
Saturated fat **1g.**
Sodium **472mg.**

36 wonton wrappers (about 8 oz.)
4 cups unsalted chicken or duck stock
watercress sprigs for garnish
Duckling-scallion filling
8 oz. duck breast meat or turkey thigh meat, finely chopped
2 tbsp. dry sherry
1 tbsp. Chinese black vinegar or balsamic vinegar
1 egg white
1 garlic clove, finely chopped
¼ cup chopped scallions (about 2)
1 tbsp. hoisin sauce
6 tbsp. chopped water chestnuts
2 dried shiitake or Chinese black mushrooms, soaked in very hot water for 20 minutes, drained, stemmed, squeezed dry and chopped
2 tbsp. cloud-ear mushrooms, soaked and very finely chopped
freshly ground black pepper
Ginger-plum sauce
32 oz. canned purple plums in heavy syrup, drained
1 tbsp. cornstarch, mixed with 2 tbsp. water
1 tsp. finely chopped fresh ginger
1 garlic clove, finely chopped
1 cup unsalted chicken or duck stock
1 tbsp. low-sodium soy sauce
1 tbsp. rice vinegar
¼ tsp. salt

Combine the filling ingredients in a large bowl.

To prepare the ginger-plum sauce, first remove the pits and skins from the plums, then mash their flesh with a fork (there should be about 1 cup of flesh). Put the flesh in a saucepan over medium heat and stir in the cornstarch mixture. Add the remaining sauce ingredients and stir constantly until the sauce boils and thickens. Set the sauce aside.

Place about 1½ teaspoons of the filling mixture in the center of a wonton wrapper. Using your fingers or a pastry brush, apply a thin film of water to two adjacent edges of the wrapper. Fold the wrapper into the shape of a wonton as demonstrated below. Repeat the process with the remaining filling and wrappers, keeping the finished dumplings and unused wrappers covered with a damp towel to prevent their drying out.

Pour enough of the 4 cups of stock into a large, shallow pan to fill it about 1 inch deep. Bring the stock to a simmer, then gently add a batch of the dumplings ▶

Shaping Wontons

1 *MOISTENING THE EDGES. Place the filling in the center of a wonton square. Moisten a fingertip with water and run it along two adjacent edges of the wrapper. Keep the other wrappers stacked as you work to prevent drying.*

2 *SEALING THE EDGES. Fold the dry edges over the wet ones slightly off center to form two points. Then press the edges together with your fingertips to seal the wonton. Alternatively, the edges may be matched to form a single triangle.*

3 *FINISHING THE WONTON. Moisten the left corner of the triangle. Bring the right corner over the left corner, and squeeze the two together to plump up the filling and to get the corners to stick. Set the wonton aside and fill the other wrappers.*

to the liquid. The dumplings should form a single layer, with their sides barely touching, and the stock should cover them by about ½ inch. When the stock returns to a simmer, partially cover the pan and cook the dumplings for eight minutes.

With a slotted spoon, transfer the dumplings to a heated platter. Cover the dumplings with aluminum foil to keep them warm while you cook the remaining dumplings, adding more stock to the skillet if necessary. Reheat the sauce.

Arrange half a dozen dumplings on each of six warmed plates. Garnish each with watercress sprigs. Serve immediately, passing the sauce separately.

EDITOR'S NOTE: *Both the filling and the sauce may be prepared up to 24 hours in advance and refrigerated until you are ready to use them.*

Broccoli spears stir fried in ginger, soy sauce and sesame oil make a colorful accompaniment to the dumplings.

Barbecue-Pork Noodles with Emeralds and Rubies

Serves 4
Working (and total) time: 25 minutes

Calories **377**
Protein **33g.**
Cholesterol **45mg.**
Total fat **16g.**
Saturated fat **4g.**
Sodium **553mg.**

12 oz. fresh Asian egg noodles, or 8 oz. dried vermicelli
1 tbsp. safflower oil
8 oz. Chinese barbecue pork, trimmed of all fat and thinly sliced into pieces about 1 inch square
1 tbsp. finely chopped fresh ginger
1 cup snow peas, strings removed, sliced diagonally
1 red bell pepper, seeded, deribbed and sliced lengthwise
1½ cups fresh bean sprouts, rinsed and drained
8 dried shiitake or Chinese black mushrooms, soaked in very hot water for 20 minutes, stemmed and sliced, the soaking liquid reduced to ¼ cup and reserved
½ cup unsalted chicken stock
2 tbsp. low-sodium soy sauce

Add the noodles to 4 quarts of boiling water with 2 teaspoons of salt. Start testing them after three minutes and cook them until they are *al dente*. Drain the noodles and keep them warm.

Heat the oil in a hot wok or a heavy-bottomed skillet over medium-high heat. Add the pork and ginger and stir fry them for two minutes. Add the snow peas, pepper slices, bean sprouts and mushrooms, and continue to stir fry the mixture until the snow peas turn bright green — about two minutes more.

Remove the pork and vegetables from the pan and set them aside. Add the drained noodles, the reserved mushroom-soaking liquid, the stock and soy sauce to the pan. Toss the noodles to combine them with the liquid. Return the pork and vegetables to the pan and mix gently. Divide the noodles among four large soup bowls and ladle over them any liquid remaining in the pan. Serve immediately.

EDITOR'S NOTE: *Barbecue pork is a product available in Asian specialty markets. If unavailable, it can be made at home by marinating an 8-ounce piece of boneless pork loin, quartered lengthwise, in a mixture of ½ tablespoon low-sodium soy sauce, ½ tablespoon dry sherry, ½ teaspoon dark sesame oil, ½ teaspoon finely chopped fresh ginger, ½ tablespoon honey and 1 finely chopped garlic clove. Refrigerate the pork strips in the marinade for eight hours or overnight. Then attach each strip to a paper clip unfolded into an S shape, reserving the marinade, and hook the clips onto an oven rack; insert the rack at its highest position in a preheated 350° F. oven. Set a pan of water below the strips to catch their dripping juices, and roast the strips for 45 minutes. Baste the strips with the remaining marinade, raise the heat to 425° F. and roast them for 20 minutes more.*

Spicy Noodles with Pork and Peanuts

Serves 4
Working time: about 30 minutes
Total time: about 1 hour

Calories **318**
Protein **25g.**
Cholesterol **22mg.**
Total fat **15g.**
Saturated fat **4g.**
Sodium **526mg.**

12 oz. fresh Asian egg noodles, or 8 oz. dried linguine
1 tbsp. safflower oil
2 scallions, finely chopped
2 tsp. very finely chopped fresh ginger
1 garlic clove, finely chopped
¼ to ½ tsp. crushed red pepper or sambal oelek
6 oz. boneless pork, trimmed of all fat, finely chopped with a knife or in a food processor
2 tbsp. dry sherry
1 tsp. bean paste
1 tsp. hoisin sauce
1 tbsp. low-sodium soy sauce
¼ cup unsalted chicken stock
¼ cup diced water chestnuts
¼ cup dry-roasted unsalted peanuts, coarsely chopped
¼ tsp. dark sesame oil
1 tbsp. chopped cilantro
1 cucumber, halved, seeded and julienned
½ cup fresh bean sprouts
¼ cup shredded or julienned red radishes
1 apple, peeled, sliced and tossed with 2 tsp. lemon juice

Add the noodles to 3 quarts of boiling water. Start testing them after three minutes and cook them until they are *al dente*. Drain the noodles, rinse them under cold water and set them aside.

Heat the safflower oil in a hot wok or a large, heavy-bottomed skillet over high heat. Add the scallions, ginger, garlic and the crushed red pepper or sambal oelek, and stir fry for 30 seconds. Add the pork and continue stir frying until the pork is no longer pink — about three minutes. Pour in the sherry along with the bean paste,

hoisin sauce and soy sauce, then add the stock and the water chestnuts. Cook for two minutes before stirring in the peanuts and sesame oil. Add the noodles and toss them with the sauce until they are heated through — about one minute.

Transfer the noodles to a serving dish. Scatter the cilantro over the top and garnish the dish with the cucumber, bean sprouts, radishes and apple. Alternatively, the garnishes may be served separately in small bowls so that each diner may choose his own.

Four-Season Dumplings with Sweet-and-Sour Sauce

Serves 6 as an appetizer
Working (and total) time: about 1 hour and 30 minutes

Calories **150**
Protein **12g.**
Cholesterol **25mg.**
Total fat **4g.**
Saturated fat **1g.**
Sodium **201mg.**

6 oz. gyoza wrappers, or 6 oz. wonton wrappers cut into rounds
6 oz. lean pork, trimmed of all fat and finely chopped
2 oz. shrimp, peeled and finely chopped
1 tbsp. dry sherry
2 tsp. grated fresh ginger
1 garlic clove, very finely chopped
3 scallions, trimmed and very finely chopped
½ cup grated sweet potato or carrot
2 tsp. low-sodium soy sauce
½ tsp. fresh lemon juice
2 tsp. very finely chopped cilantro
¼ cup water chestnuts, diced
2 dried shiitake or Chinese black mushrooms, soaked in very hot water for 20 minutes, stems removed, cut into ¼-inch squares
⅛ red bell pepper, seeded, deribbed and cut into ¼-inch squares
2 tbsp. green peas
Sweet-and-sour sauce
3 tbsp. frozen tangerine-juice concentrate or orange-juice concentrate
¼ cup unsalted chicken stock
2 tbsp. fresh lemon juice
2 tbsp. rice vinegar
1 tbsp. oyster sauce
1 tbsp. sugar
1 tbsp. unsalted tomato paste
2 tsp. cornstarch

Combine the sauce ingredients in a small pan and stir them together until the cornstarch is dissolved. Bring the sauce to a boil, stirring constantly until it thickens. Set the pan aside.

To make the filling, combine the pork, shrimp, sherry, ginger, garlic, scallions, sweet potato or carrot, soy sauce, lemon juice, cilantro and three fourths of the water chestnuts in a large bowl. Place a scant teaspoon of the filling in the center of a gyoza or wonton wrapper and form it into a dumpling (technique, page 127). Garnish each of the four openings with one piece each of mushroom, red pepper, green peas and the remaining water chestnuts.

Using a paper towel or a pastry brush, lightly oil the floor of a steamer. Arrange as many of the dumplings inside as will fit without touching. Cover the steamer, set it in a pot filled with 1 inch of boiling water, and steam the dumplings over high heat for eight minutes. Remove the dumplings and set them aside on a tray or serving platter; cover them with aluminum foil and put them in a low oven to keep them warm. Cook the remaining dumplings the same way, oiling the steamer floor before adding each new batch.

Meanwhile, rewarm the dipping sauce over low heat, stirring occasionally. Serve the dumplings hot; pass the dipping sauce separately.

EDITOR'S NOTE: *To make a simpler variation of the dumpling, pull the outside edges of the filled wrapper in toward the center, creating a cup; place a piece of each garnish inside the cup and steam the dumplings as directed.*

Fashioning Four-Season Dumplings

1 *SHAPING THE PIECE. Place the filling in the center of a gyoza wrapper or a wonton wrapper cut into a circle. Bring two edges of the circle together and pinch them at the top. Do the same with the other edges. Using a pastry brush or your finger, moisten the dough to make them stick, if necessary.*

2 *ADDING THE VEGETABLES. Flare out the openings. Drop a different vegetable filling into each. Repeat these steps to fill the remaining wrappers; then gently steam the dumplings.*

Ma Po Sichuan Noodles

Serves 4
Working (and total) time: about 25 minutes

Calories **306**
Protein **27g.**
Cholesterol **30mg.**
Total fat **13g.**
Saturated fat **3g.**
Sodium **469mg.**

8 oz. thin, dried wheat noodles or linguine
8 oz. lean pork, trimmed of all fat and diced
2 tsp. fermented black beans, rinsed and drained
2 tbsp. dry sherry
2 tsp. finely chopped fresh garlic
4 scallions, thinly sliced (about ½ cup)
6 dried shiitake or Chinese black mushrooms, soaked in very hot water for 20 minutes, drained, stemmed and diced, the soaking liquid reserved
2 tsp. hoisin sauce
2 tsp. low-sodium soy sauce
1 to 2 tsp. chili paste with garlic
1 cup unsalted chicken stock, reduced to ½ cup
1 tsp. cornstarch
1 tbsp. safflower oil
½ tsp. dark sesame oil

Combine the pork with the black beans, sherry, garlic and half of the scallions. Let the pork marinate for 10 minutes. Meanwhile, in a large saucepan combine the mushrooms, their soaking liquid, the hoisin sauce, soy sauce, chili paste, and all but 1 tablespoon of the reduced chicken stock. Heat the mixture to a simmer.

Add the noodles to 4 quarts of boiling water. Start testing the noodles after three minutes and cook them until they are *al dente.*

Drain the noodles and combine them with the stock-and-mushroom mixture. Combine the cornstarch with the reserved tablespoon of stock. Add this mixture to the noodles and simmer them for three minutes.

Heat the safflower oil in a hot wok or a deep, heavy-bottomed skillet over high heat; add the pork mixture and stir fry it for about one minute. Turn off the heat, add the noodles and sesame oil to the pork mixture, and toss well. Arrange the noodles on a heated serving platter and garnish them with the remaining scallions. Serve immediately, or at room temperature.

Japanese Summer Noodles with Shrimp

Serves 6
Working (and total) time: about 45 minutes

Calories **199**
Protein **11g.**
Cholesterol **41mg.**
Total fat **1g.**
Saturated fat **0g.**
Sodium **224mg.**

8 oz. somen, or capellini or vermicelli
18 medium shrimp, peeled, the tails left on and the shells reserved
1 slice fresh ginger, about ⅛ inch thick
1 tbsp. low-sodium soy sauce
3 tbsp. mirin (sweetened Japanese rice wine)
6 dried shiitake or Chinese black mushrooms, rinsed
Garnish
watercress sprigs
2 scallions, thinly sliced diagonally, rinsed under cold water and drained
2 tbsp. grated fresh ginger
2 tbsp. wasabi (Japanese horseradish paste), made by mixing enough water with 1 ½ tbsp. wasabi powder to form a stiff paste

Bring 2 cups of water to a boil in a saucepan. Add the shrimp and the slice of ginger. Cover the pan, remove it from the heat and let it stand for five minutes. Strain the resulting stock into a second saucepan, reserving the shrimp and discarding the ginger. Add the shrimp shells to the stock and bring the liquid to a boil. Simmer the stock for 15 minutes, then strain it through cheese-cloth back into the first pan. Discard the shells. Reduce the stock to about ½ cup and let it cool. Combine the stock with the soy sauce and 1 tablespoon of the mirin, and divide this dipping sauce among six small bowls.

In a saucepan, pour 1½ cups of boiling water over the mushrooms and let them soak for 10 minutes. Add the remaining 2 tablespoons of mirin and simmer until almost all of the liquid has evaporated — approximately 20 minutes. As soon as the mushrooms are cool enough to handle, remove their stems; cut the mushrooms in half, taking care not to squeeze out the liquid they have absorbed.

Add the somen to 1½ quarts of boiling water; start testing the noodles after two minutes and cook them until they are *al dente.* Drain the somen, rinse them under cold water, and set aside in a bowl of cold water.

To serve, divide the noodles among six individual glass bowls. Put two or three ice cubes in each bowl, then pour in enough ice water (about ½ cup) to float the noodles. Arrange three shrimp and two mushroom halves on top of each portion of noodles. Garnish the bowls with the watercress and scallions. For each serving, place a bowl of noodles, a teaspoon of the grated ginger and a dab of wasabi on a large plate, with a bowl of the dipping sauce alongside.

EDITOR'S NOTE: *If you have access to a Japanese market, substitute ½ cup of dashi — an infusion of dried kelp and bonito shavings — for the ½ cup of shrimp stock in the dipping sauce.*

4 Topped with tomato sauce and redolent of fresh herbs, a slice of lasagne cooked by microwave reveals layers of spinach and cheese (recipe, page 131).

Pasta in the Microwave Oven

Lasagne Layered with Spinach

Serves 8
Working time: about 20 minutes
Total time: about 1 hour and 15 minutes

Calories **302**
Protein **20g.**
Cholesterol **41mg.**
Total fat **13g.**
Saturated fat **8g.**
Sodium **412mg.**

8 lasagne
2 tbsp. unsalted butter
1 medium onion, finely chopped (about 1 cup)
2 garlic cloves, finely chopped
4 oz. mushrooms, wiped clean and thinly sliced
28 oz. canned unsalted tomatoes, drained and coarsely chopped, the juice reserved
4 tbsp. unsalted tomato paste
¼ cup red wine
1 tbsp. chopped fresh oregano, or ½ tbsp. dried oregano
2 tbsp. chopped fresh basil leaves, or 1 tbsp. dried basil
2 tbsp. dark brown sugar
½ tsp. salt
freshly ground black pepper
2 tbsp. freshly grated Parmesan cheese
1 lb. part-skim ricotta cheese
1 egg white
1 lb. fresh spinach, rinsed, stemmed, blanched in boiling water for 1 minute, squeezed dry and chopped
8 oz. part-skim mozzarella, thinly sliced

Microwaving might seem an inappropriate way to cook pasta. After all, does not pasta require lots of water to cook well? But the fact is that some pasta can be microwaved in relatively little water — or without any water at all when sauce or stock is substituted.

The trick is to provide just enough moisture for the pasta to absorb. The moisture renders it supple and produces the desired *al dente* quality of the boiled product. But the cook still must check for doneness to avoid having the pasta turn soft and sticky. And remember that the food will go on cooking for several minutes after you have removed it from the oven.

The nine recipes that follow indicate precisely how much sauce, stock or water to include. (When cooking the pasta in water, be sure to use a deep enough dish so that the water will not boil over, and be careful not to burn yourself in the steam as you stir the contents, or on the hot dish as you remove it from the oven.) Some of the sauces can be prepared in advance in the microwave and added later.

Anyone who does not like having a big pot of water boiling away on the stove, especially on a hot and muggy summer's day, will welcome the microwaving method. And in the two recipes that call for the sauce and pasta to cook together, there will be fewer dishes to clean up afterward, and time will be saved as well, since the pasta need not be precooked.

Once cooks discover the ease of working with dried manicotti tubes and lasagne (both of which tear all too readily when cooked conventionally), they may well become converted to the microwave technique. The cheese and sauce are spread on the lasagne before the pasta is cooked; the manicotti are prestuffed and sauced. The proof, of course, is in the trying: You'll find recipes for lasagne layered with fresh spinach and for manicotti filled with a three-cheese and parsley combination on pages 131 and 138 respectively.

The recipes have been tested in both 625-watt and 700-watt ovens. Though power settings often vary among different manufacturers' ovens, the recipes use "high" to indicate 100 percent power, "medium high" for 70 percent and "medium" for 50 percent.

To begin the sauce, put the butter in a 2-quart glass bowl, cover it with a lid or plastic wrap, and microwave it on high until the butter is melted — about one minute. Add the onion, garlic and mushrooms, and toss them until they are coated with the butter. Cover the bowl again and microwave it on medium high (70 percent power) for two minutes. Add the tomatoes, the reserved juice, the tomato paste, wine, oregano, basil, sugar, salt and some pepper, and stir well. Cover the bowl with a paper towel and microwave the contents on high for 12 minutes, stirring every four minutes. Stir in the Parmesan cheese and set the mixture aside.

In a smaller bowl, mix the ricotta with the egg white and some more pepper. Add the spinach and mix well.

Assemble the lasagne in a 10-inch-square shallow baking dish. First spread ½ cup of the sauce evenly over the bottom of the dish. Lay four uncooked lasagne noodles side by side in the sauce, then cover them with a thin layer of the spinach mixture and a layer of mozzarella slices. Repeat the layering process: Spread half of the remaining sauce atop the cheese, then cover it ▶

with the remaining lasagne, the rest of the spinach mixture and the last of the mozzarella. Top the dish with the remaining sauce and cover it with plastic wrap; microwave it on high for six minutes, then on medium high (70 percent power) for 20 minutes more. Let the lasagne stand for 15 minutes before serving it.

Couscous with Lamb and Apricots

Serves 4
Working time: about 15 minutes
Total time: about 25 minutes

Calories **512**
Protein **25g.**
Cholesterol **81mg.**
Total fat **30g.**
Saturated fat **14g.**
Sodium **374mg.**

1 cup couscous
2 tbsp. white wine vinegar
½ tsp. salt
¾ lb. ground lamb
1 small onion, finely chopped (about ½ cup)
2 garlic cloves, finely chopped
2 tbsp. chopped fresh tarragon, or 2 tsp. dried tarragon
freshly ground black pepper
⅓ cup unsalted tomato juice
1 small green pepper, seeded, deribbed and sliced lengthwise into narrow strips (about ½ cup)
½ cup dried apricots (about 8 apricots), cut in half, soaked in ½ cup hot water for 5 minutes, then drained
2 tbsp. toasted pine nuts

In a 1-quart measuring cup or a glass bowl covered with a lid or plastic wrap, microwave 1½ cups of hot water on high until it boils — about three minutes. Add the couscous, the vinegar and ¼ teaspoon of the salt, and stir well. Cover the container again and let it stand until all the liquid is absorbed — about five minutes.

Meanwhile, in a large bowl, combine the lamb, onion, garlic, tarragon, the remaining ¼ teaspoon of salt, some pepper and the tomato juice. Blend these ingredients well; with your hands, form the mixture into nuggets about 1 inch in diameter. Put the nuggets in a shallow baking dish, and scatter the green pepper and apricots over the top. Cover the dish with a paper towel and microwave it on high for seven minutes, stopping after four minutes to stir the mixture.

Test the lamb for doneness by dividing a nugget with a fork; if it is still pink inside, microwave the dish on high for another minute and test again. When the lamb is thoroughly cooked, drain off the excess liquid. Put the couscous in the dish with the lamb nuggets and toss well. Transfer the mixture to a platter, top it with the pine nuts, and serve immediately.

Pasta Shells with Clams and Corn

BEFORE STEAMING THE CLAMS, DISCARD ANY THAT
FAIL TO CLOSE WHEN THEY ARE TAPPED.

Serves 4
Working (and total) time: about 40 minutes

Calories **357**
Protein **17g.**
Cholesterol **37mg.**
Total fat **8g.**
Saturated fat **4g.**
Sodium **134mg.**

8 oz. medium pasta shells
16 littleneck or cherrystone clams, the shells scrubbed
1½ tbsp. unsalted butter
2 scallions, sliced diagonally into thin ovals
½ cup fresh corn kernels, or ½ cup frozen corn kernels, defrosted
3 tbsp. unbleached all-purpose flour
⅔ cup low-fat milk
1 tbsp. paprika, preferably Hungarian
⅛ tsp. cayenne pepper
2 tbsp. freshly grated Parmesan cheese

Pour ¼ cup of water into a 2-quart bowl. Cover the bowl with a lid or plastic wrap and microwave it on high for one minute. Add the clams, cover the bowl again and microwave it on high until the clams have partially opened — about two minutes. Discard any clams that remain closed. Pour off and discard the water and leave the clams to cool.

Pour 5 cups of hot water into another 2-quart bowl.

Cover the bowl and microwave it on high until the water comes to a boil — about seven minutes. Remove the cover, taking care to avoid the steam; add ½ teaspoon of salt and the pasta shells to the water. Replace the cover, leaving a small opening to vent the steam, and microwave the pasta on high for two minutes. Uncover the bowl, stir the pasta and replace the cover, again creating a vent. Return the bowl to the oven. Microwave it on medium (50 percent power) until the shells are *al dente* — about five minutes more. Drain the pasta thoroughly and set it aside.

Put the butter in a 1-quart bowl and microwave it on high for one minute. Add the scallions and corn, cover the bowl, and microwave it on high for one minute.

Shuck the clams over their bowl to catch any juices. Allow the sediment from the clams to settle to the bottom of the bowl. Pour off ½ cup of the clam liquid and reserve it; discard the rest. Let the clams stand while you finish the sauce.

Whisk the flour into the scallion-corn mixture, forming a paste. Gradually pour in the milk and the reserved clam liquid, stirring until the paste dissolves. Stir in the paprika and cayenne pepper. Cover the bowl and microwave it on high for 90 seconds. Uncover the bowl, stir the mixture, then replace the cover and microwave it on high for 90 seconds more.

Put the pasta shells and clams in a serving bowl. Pour the sauce over them and toss well. Cover the bowl and microwave it on high for one minute, then sprinkle the cheese over the pasta and serve at once.

Egg Noodles with Beef and Mushrooms in a Creamy Sauce

THIS RECIPE IS A LOW-CALORIE VARIATION OF
THE CLASSIC BEEF STROGANOFF.

Serves 4
Working (and total) time: about 20 minutes

Calories **433**
Protein **26g.**
Cholesterol **98mg.**
Total fat **14g.**
Saturated fat **7g.**
Sodium **444mg.**

8 oz. wide egg noodles
2 tsp. safflower oil
1 tbsp. unsalted butter
8 oz. mushrooms, wiped clean, stems trimmed, thinly sliced
1 small onion, thinly sliced, the layers separated (about ¾ cup)
8 oz. beef tenderloin, cut into thin strips about 2 inches long and ½ inch wide
1 garlic clove, finely chopped
1 tsp. dry mustard, mixed with 1 tsp. water
1½ tbsp. paprika, preferably Hungarian
½ tsp. salt
freshly ground black pepper
¼ cup sour cream
½ cup plain low-fat yogurt
¼ cup chives, coarsely chopped

Cook the noodles in the conventional manner: Put them into 3 quarts of boiling water on the stove top with 1½ teaspoons of salt. Start testing the noodles after seven minutes and cook them until they are *al dente*. Drain the noodles, toss them with the oil, and set them aside.

While the noodles are cooking, put the butter in a 2-quart bowl and cover the bowl with a lid or plastic wrap. Microwave the butter on high for 30 seconds. Add the mushrooms and onion, and gently toss them until they are coated with the butter. Cover the bowl again and microwave the contents on medium high (70 percent power) for two minutes. Add the beef strips, garlic, mustard, 1 tablespoon of the paprika, the ½ teaspoon of salt and a generous grinding of black pepper to the mushroom-onion mixture. Cover the bowl again and microwave the contents on medium high (70 percent power) for five minutes, stirring the mixture halfway through the cooking time. Remove the bowl and drain off the liquid that has accumulated in the bottom.

Add the noodles, stock, sour cream and yogurt to the bowl; stir well, cover the bowl and microwave it on high for two minutes, stirring after one minute. Transfer the mixture to a serving platter. Sprinkle the remaining ½ tablespoon of paprika and the chives over the top and serve the dish hot.

Penne with Provençal Vegetables

Serves 4
Working (and total) time: about 40 minutes

Calories **336**
Protein **11g.**
Cholesterol **1mg.**
Total fat **7g.**
Saturated fat **1g.**
Sodium **185mg.**

8 oz. penne (or other short, tubular pasta)
1 small eggplant (about ½ lb.)
2 zucchini
2 red peppers, seeded, deribbed and cut into ½-inch squares
3 garlic cloves, peeled and thinly sliced
2 tbsp. chopped fresh parsley
¼ tsp. fresh oregano, or ⅛ tsp. dried oregano
¼ tsp. finely chopped fresh rosemary, or ⅛ tsp. dried rosemary, crushed
¼ tsp. fresh thyme, or ⅛ tsp. dried thyme leaves
⅛ tsp. fennel seeds
¼ tsp. salt
freshly ground black pepper
2 tbsp. virgin olive oil
2 cups unsalted chicken stock
1 cup unsalted tomato juice

Halve the eggplant and the zucchini lengthwise, then cut them lengthwise again into wedges about ½ inch wide. Slice the wedges into 1-inch-long pieces. Put the pieces in a baking dish along with the red pepper, garlic, parsley, oregano, rosemary, thyme, fennel seeds, salt and some pepper. Cover the dish and microwave it on high for two minutes. Rotate the dish half a turn and microwave it on high until the vegetables are barely tender — about two minutes more. Stir in the oil and set the mixture aside while you cook the pasta.

In a deep bowl, combine the penne, stock and tomato juice. If necessary, add just enough water to immerse the pasta in liquid. Cover the bowl and microwave it on high, rotating the bowl a quarter turn and stirring the pasta every two minutes, until it is *al dente* — about 15 minutes in all. With a slotted spoon, transfer the pasta to the baking dish with the vegetable mixture and stir to combine. Pour about half of the pasta-cooking liquid into the dish, then cover the dish and microwave it on high for two minutes more to heat it through. Serve at once.

Green Fettuccine
with Flounder

Serves 4
Working (and total) time: about 25 minutes

Calories **329**
Protein **19g.**
Cholesterol **30mg.**
Total fat **6g.**
Saturated fat **1g.**
Sodium **327mg.**

8 oz. green fettuccine
4 tsp. virgin olive oil
2 garlic cloves, peeled and finely chopped
1 tbsp. chopped fresh oregano
14 oz. unsalted canned whole tomatoes, drained and coarsely chopped
½ cup clam juice
½ lb. fillet of flounder, cut into bite-size pieces
¼ tsp. salt
freshly ground black pepper
2 tbsp. freshly grated Parmesan cheese

Pour 5 cups of hot water into a 2-quart glass bowl. Cover the bowl with a lid or plastic wrap and micro-wave it on high until the water comes to a boil — about six minutes. Stir in ½ teaspoon of salt and add the fettuccine; cover the bowl again and microwave it on high, stirring once after three minutes, until the pasta is *al dente* — about six minutes in all. Drain the fettuc-cine, then toss it with 2 teaspoons of the oil and set it aside in a microwave-safe serving dish.

In a shallow 1-quart dish, combine the remaining 2 teaspoons of oil with the garlic, oregano and toma-toes. Cover the bowl with a lid or plastic wrap and microwave the mixture on medium high (70 percent power) until it is heated through — about 90 seconds. Uncover the dish and stir in the clam juice and the flounder; cover the dish again and microwave it on high until the flounder is cooked through and can be easily flaked with a fork — two to three minutes.

Pour the fish mixture over the fettuccine, season with the ¼ teaspoon of salt and some pepper, and toss well. Cover the dish and microwave it on high until it is heated through — about one minute. Sprinkle the cheese over the top and serve immediately.

Spaghetti with Garlic, Oregano and Parsley

Serves 4
Working (and total) time: about 30 minutes

Calories **290**
Protein **8g.**
Cholesterol **0mg.**
Total fat **8g.**
Saturated fat **1g.**
Sodium **240mg.**

8 oz. spaghetti
2 whole garlic bulbs, the cloves separated and peeled
¼ tsp. chopped fresh oregano, or ⅛ tsp. dried oregano
2 tbsp. chopped fresh parsley, preferably Italian
¼ tsp. salt
⅛ tsp. cayenne pepper
2 tbsp. virgin olive oil
1 lemon, cut into 8 wedges

In a baking dish, combine the garlic, oregano, parsley, salt, cayenne pepper and ½ cup of water. Cover with a lid or plastic wrap, and microwave the mixture on high for six minutes, rotating the dish every two minutes. Remove the dish from the oven and let it stand for two minutes. Purée the mixture and set it aside.

Cook the spaghetti in the conventional manner: Add it to 3 quarts of boiling water with 1½ teaspoons of salt. Start testing after 10 minutes and cook the spaghetti until it is *al dente*. Drain the pasta and return it to the pot. Pour in the oil and toss well. Add the garlic sauce and toss again. Garnish with the lemon wedges.

them with the butter, then microwave them on medium high (70 percent power) for four minutes. Add the tomatoes and their juice, the tomato paste, oregano, basil, brown sugar, some pepper and the salt, and stir well. Cover the bowl loosely and microwave the contents on medium high (70 percent power) for 12 minutes, stirring every four minutes. Set the sauce aside.

To make the filling, stir together the cottage cheese, mozzarella, egg whites, parsley and the Parmesan cheese. Using a small spoon or a pastry bag with no tip, carefully fill the tubes with the mixture.

To assemble the dish, first reheat the sauce, if necessary, then spread half of it over the bottom of a shallow baking dish. Lay the filled manicotti tubes in the sauce in a single layer and pour the remaining sauce over them. Cover the dish and microwave it on high for 10 minutes, then turn each tube over. Cover the dish again and microwave it on medium high for 17 minutes more. Uncover the dish and let the manicotti stand for 12 to 15 minutes. Garnish with sprigs of fresh basil if desired.

Manicotti with Cottage Cheese and Zucchini

TO ENSURE THAT THE PASTA WILL COOK COMPLETELY THROUGH, THE SAUCE MUST BE WARM WHEN YOU ASSEMBLE THE DISH.

Serves 6
Working time: about 35 minutes
Total time: about 1 hour and 30 minutes

Calories **381**
Protein **24g.**
Cholesterol **30mg.**
Total fat **11g.**
Saturated fat **7g.**
Sodium **592mg.**

12 manicotti tubes (about 8 oz.)
2 tbsp. unsalted butter
3 large shallots, finely chopped (about 3 tbsp.)
2 garlic cloves, finely chopped
1 medium carrot, peeled and coarsely grated (about ⅔ cup)
1 medium zucchini, sliced into thin rounds (about 1¼ cups)
28 oz. unsalted canned tomatoes, drained and coarsely chopped, the juice reserved
4 tbsp. tomato paste
1 tbsp. chopped fresh oregano, or ½ tbsp. dried oregano
2 tbsp. chopped fresh basil leaves, or 1 tbsp. dried basil
2 tbsp. dark brown sugar
freshly ground black pepper
¼ tsp. salt
¾ lb. small-curd low-fat cottage cheese
4 oz. part-skim mozzarella, coarsely grated
3 egg whites
3 tbsp. chopped fresh parsley
½ cup freshly grated Parmesan cheese
fresh basil sprigs for garnish (optional)

Put the butter in a 2-quart bowl. Cover the bowl with a lid or plastic wrap and microwave it on high until the butter melts — about 30 seconds. Add the shallots, garlic, carrot and zucchini; toss the vegetables to coat

Tomatoes Stuffed with Farfalline

Serves 4
Working time: about 15 minutes
Total time: about 30 minutes

Calories **295**
Protein **15g.**
Cholesterol **15mg.**
Total fat **11g.**
Saturated fat **6g.**
Sodium **322mg.**

½ cup farfalline (or other small, fancy pasta)
4 large, ripe tomatoes (about 1½ lb.)
2 tbsp. unsalted butter
1 small onion, chopped (about ½ cup)
½ green pepper, seeded, deribbed and chopped (about ¼ cup)
1 garlic clove, finely chopped
6 oz. lean ground beef
½ tsp. salt
freshly ground black pepper
1 tbsp. curry powder
1 tsp. paprika, preferably Hungarian
⅛ tsp. cayenne pepper
2 tsp. brown sugar

Put 1 quart of hot water and ½ teaspoon of salt in a 2-quart bowl. Cover the bowl with a lid or plastic wrap and microwave it on high until the water boils — about five minutes. Add the pasta and cover the bowl again. Microwave the pasta on high for three minutes, stirring it halfway through the cooking time. Test the pasta; if it is not yet *al dente,* microwave it for one minute more and test again. Drain the pasta and set it aside.

Remove and discard the tops of the tomatoes. With a teaspoon, scoop out the flesh of each tomato and set the cases aside. Chop the flesh, add it to the pasta, and toss well.

In a larger, covered bowl, microwave the butter on high for 30 seconds. Add the onion, green pepper and garlic, and toss them until they are coated with the butter. Cover the bowl again and microwave it on high for 90 seconds.

Crumble the beef onto a glass plate and season it with ¼ teaspoon of the salt and some black pepper. Cover the plate with a paper towel and microwave the beef on high for a total of 90 seconds, stirring after 45 seconds.

Spoon the cooked beef into the bowl with the onion mixture and discard the liquid remaining on the plate. Add the pasta-tomato mixture and the curry powder, paprika, cayenne pepper and sugar, and stir thoroughly. Season the inside of each tomato with the remaining ¼ teaspoon of salt and some black pepper. Stuff each tomato loosely with the beef-and-pasta mixture.

Arrange the stuffed tomatoes around the edge of a plate. Cover them with plastic wrap and microwave them on medium high (70 percent power) for seven minutes, turning each tomato a half turn midway through the cooking time. Remove the tomatoes from the oven and let them stand, still covered, for two minutes before serving.

Glossary

Arugula: a peppery-flavored salad plant with long, leafy stems.

Asian egg noodles: a long, toothsome wheat pasta available fresh, frozen or dried in Asian markets. Fresh noodles may be refrigerated for up to five days; when stored frozen, they should be cooked without being defrosted.

Balsamic vinegar: a mild, intensely fragrant wine-based vinegar.

Bean paste (or bean sauce): a thick brown paste made from soybeans, spices and salt.

Bean sprouts: the sprouts of green mung beans. Use only fresh bean sprouts; canned bean sprouts are often mushy.

Beanthread noodles (also called cellophane noodles, glass noodles, harusame, mung-bean noodles, saifun and transparent noodles): an Asian pasta made from various vegetable starches, most often that of mung beans. Available in forms ranging from 1-ounce skeins to 1-pound packages of loose noodles, beanthread noodles should be soaked in hot water until they are soft.

Black vinegar, Chinese (also called Chenkong vinegar, Chinkiang vinegar): a dark vinegar made from fermented rice.

Blanch: to partially cook food by briefly immersing it in boiling water.

Buckwheat: the seed of the flowering buckwheat plant. Buckwheat flour is unrelated to wheat flour and lacks the proteins required to form gluten.

Bulgur: whole-wheat kernels that have been steamed, dried and cracked.

Calorie (or kilocalorie): a unit of heat measurement, used to gauge the amount of energy a food supplies when it is broken down for use in the body.

Cardamom: the bittersweet dried seeds of a plant in the ginger family. May be used whole or ground.

Cellophane noodles: see Beanthread noodles.

Chiffonade: a leafy vegetable sliced into very thin shreds.

Chili paste: a paste made from chili peppers, salt and other ingredients; among its variations are chili paste with garlic and chili paste with black beans.

Chili pepper: a variety of hot red, yellow or green pepper. Finger-like Asian chili peppers are much hotter than Western chilies. Tiny Thai chilies are especially fiery. Fresh or dried, chili peppers contain volatile oils that can irritate the skin and eyes; they must be handled with extreme care (caution, page 33). See also Sambal oelek.

Chili sauce, Asian: see Chili paste; Hot red-pepper sauce; Sambal oelek; Sweet chili sauce.

Chinese black mushrooms: dark dried mushrooms with a deep, smoky flavor. The larger mushrooms with cracked surfaces are considered best. Like any dried mushrooms, they must be soaked and stemmed. See also Mushrooms, dried Asian.

Chinese black vinegar: see Black vinegar, Chinese.

Chinese parsley: see Cilantro.

Chinese sausage: a small, thin, hard sausage available in Asian markets. It should be steamed or simmered before use. To store Chinese sausage, refrigerate it for up to one month or freeze it. Chinese pork sausage — lop cheong — tastes sweetly savory.

Cholesterol: a waxy, fatlike substance that is manu-factured in the human body and is also found in foods of animal origin. Although a certain amount of cholesterol is necessary for the body to function properly, an excess can accumulate in the arteries, contributing to heart disease. See also Monounsaturated fat; Polyunsaturated fat; Saturated fat.

Cilantro (also called fresh coriander and Chinese parsley): the fresh leaves of the coriander plant; cilantro imparts a lemony, pleasingly pungent flavor to many Latin American, Indian and Asian dishes. Its leaves resemble those of flat-leaved parsley.

Citrus leaves (lime leaves): the leaves of the kaffir lime tree, used in Southeast Asian cuisine for their distinctive flavor. Citrus leaves are available fresh, frozen and dried in Asian markets; if you cannot find any, substitute fresh lime or lemon leaves, lime juice or lime zest.

Cloud-ear mushrooms (also called tree ears, tree fungus, mo-er and wood ears): silver-edged, flavorless lichen used primarily for their crunchy texture and dark color. Cloud ears expand much more than other mushrooms when soaked. See also Mushrooms, dried Asian.

Coconut milk, unsweetened: a liquid extracted from fresh or dried coconut meat. Unsweetened coconut milk can be purchased either canned or frozen. Because of its high saturated-fat content, coconut milk should be used sparingly.

Coriander: an herb whose earthy-tasting seeds are often used in curries. See also Cilantro.

Couscous: a fine-grained semolina pasta, traditionally served with the classic North African stew of the same name.

Cumin: the seeds of a plant related to caraway. The raw seeds add a pleasantly bitter flavor to curry and chili powders; when toasted, they have a nutty taste.

Dark sesame oil: a dark seasoning oil made from toasted sesame seeds, high in polyunsaturated fats, with a nutty, smoky aroma. Because the oil has a relatively low smoking point, it is rarely heated.

Fat: a basic component of many foods, comprising three types of fatty acids — saturated, monounsaturated and polyunsaturated — in varying proportions. See also Monounsaturated fat; Polyunsaturated fat; Saturated fat.

Fennel (also called Florence fennel or finocchio): a vegetable with feathery green tops and a thick, bulbous stalk. It has a milky, licorice flavor and can be eaten raw or cooked. The tops are used both as a garnish and as a flavoring. Fennel is sometimes incorrectly labeled as anise.

Fennel seeds: the aromatic dried seeds from herb fennel, a relative of vegetable fennel; used as a licorice-flavored seasoning in many Italian dishes. It is also used in curries and to make Chinese five-spice powder.

Fermented black beans: soybeans that have been fermented, dried and salted. The beans should be rinsed and crushed before use.

Fish sauce (also called nuoc mam and nam pla): a thin, brown, salty liquid made from fermented fish. It is used in Southeast Asian cooking to bring out the flavors of a dish. If fish sauce is not available, substitute a mixture of one part anchovy paste to four parts water.

Ginger: the spicy, buff-colored, rootlike stem of the ginger plant, used as a seasoning either fresh or dried and powdered. The dried form should never be substituted for the fresh.

Glass noodles: see Beanthread noodles.

Gluten: a tough network of protein strands formed when the proteins in flour link with water.

Gyoza wrappers: circular wonton wrappers.

Harusame: Japanese for beanthread noodles; the name means "spring rain." See also Beanthread noodles.

Hoisin sauce: a thick, dark, reddish brown sauce generally made from soybeans, flour, garlic, sugar and spices. It is best known as the accompaniment to Peking duck and mushi pork.

Hot red-pepper sauce: a hot, unsweetened chili sauce, such as Tabasco or the Thai sriracha sauce.

Julienne: to slice into matchstick-size pieces.

Kasha: toasted buckwheat groats. See also Buckwheat.

Lemon grass (citronella): a long, woody, lemon-flavored stalk that is shaped like a scallion. Lemon grass is available in Asian markets. To store it, refrigerate it in plastic wrap for up to two weeks; lemon grass may also be frozen for storage.

Mifun: see Rice noodles.

Mirin: a sweetened Japanese cooking wine that is made from rice. If mirin is unavailable, substitute a mixture of equal parts sugar and sake, dry sherry or white wine.

Monounsaturated fat: one of the three components of food fat. Monounsaturated fats are believed not to raise the level of cholesterol in the blood. Some oils high in monounsaturated fats — olive oil, for example — may even lower the cholesterol level.

Mung-bean noodles: see Beanthread noodles.

Mushrooms, dried Asian: Before use, dried Asian mushrooms must be soaked in very hot or boiling water for at least 20 minutes, then trimmed of their woody stems. To use the mushroom-soaking liquid as a flavoring agent, pour off and reserve the clear liquid; discard any sand that settles to the bottom. Soaked mushrooms can be stored in plastic wrap in the refrigerator. See also Chinese black mushrooms; Cloud-ear mushrooms; Shiitake mushrooms; Straw mushrooms.

Nonreactive pan: a cooking vessel whose surface does not react chemically with food.

Olive oil: any of various grades of cooking oil extracted from olives. Extra virgin olive oil has a full, fruity flavor and very low acidity. Virgin olive oil is lighter in flavor and slightly higher in acidity. Pure olive oil, a processed blend of olive oils, has the lightest taste and the highest acidity. To prevent rancidity, the oil should be stored in a cool, dark place.

Oyster sauce: a savory sauce made from oyster extract and seasonings, used to impart a subtle richness in Chinese dishes.

Pine nuts (also called pignoli): seeds from the cone of the stone pine, a tree native to the Mediterranean. Pine nuts are used in pesto and other sauces; their buttery flavor can be heightened by light toasting.

Polyunsaturated fat: one of the three types of fat found in foods, existing in abundance in such vegetable oils as safflower, sunflower, corn and soybean.

Polyunsaturated fats lower the level of cholesterol in the blood.

Radicchio: red chicory.

Recommended Dietary Allowance (RDA): the average required daily amount of an essential nutrient as determined for groups of healthy people of various ages by the National Research Council.

Reduce: to boil down a liquid in order to concentrate its flavor and thicken its consistency.

Refresh: to rinse a vegetable under cold water in order to arrest its cooking and set its color.

Rice noodles (also called mifun): an Asian pasta made from rice starch. Rice noodles are available as flat noodles, as thin vermicelli (also called rice sticks), as squares, or as wrappers called rice papers. All but rice papers must be soaked in very hot water or boiled; rice papers need only be dipped in warm water to soften them.

Rice vinegar: a mild, fragrant vinegar that is less assertive than cider vinegar and not as harsh as distilled white vinegar. It is available in dark, light, seasoned and sweetened varieties. Japanese rice vinegar is generally milder than the Chinese variety.

Rice wine: Chinese rice wine (shao-hsing) is brewed from rice and wine. Japanese rice wine (sake) has a different flavor, but it may be used as a substitute. If rice wine is unavailable, use dry sherry in its place. See also Mirin.

Safflower oil: a vegetable oil that contains a high proportion of polyunsaturated fats.

Saffron: the dried, yellowish red stigmas (or threads) of the flower of *Crocus sativus,* yielding a slightly bitter flavor and a brilliant yellow color.

Saifun: see Beanthread noodles.

Sambal oelek: an Indonesian sauce made from chili peppers. It is available in Asian markets. Sambal oelek makes an excellent substitute for fresh or dried chili peppers.

Saturated fat: one of the three components of food fat. Found in abundance in animal products and in coconut and palm oils, saturated fats raise the level of cholesterol in the blood. Because high blood-cholesterol levels may contribute to heart disease, saturated-fat consumption should be held to less than 10 percent of the calories consumed each day.

Sauté: to cook a food quickly in a small amount of oil over high heat.

Scallions (also called green onions and spring onions): a slender relative of the onion, with white bases supporting elongated green leaves.

Semolina: the ground endosperm of kernels of durum wheat. Semolina flour makes a pasta of excellent resilience and body.

Sesame oil: see Dark sesame oil.

Shiitake mushrooms: a variety of mushroom, originally cultivated only in Japan, that is sold fresh or dried. Dried shiitake mushrooms should be soaked and stemmed before they are used. See also Mushrooms, dried Asian.

Snow peas: small, flat green pea pods, eaten whole, with only the stems and strings removed. If fresh snow peas are unavailable, substitute sugar-snap peas or thinly sliced broccoli stems; frozen snow peas tend to be soggy.

Sodium: a nutrient essential to maintaining the proper balance of fluids in the body. In most diets, a major source of the element is table salt, made up of 40 percent sodium. Excess sodium may cause high blood pressure, a contributor to heart disease. One teaspoon of salt, with 2,132 milligrams of sodium, contains about two thirds of the maximum ''safe and adequate'' daily sodium intake recommended by the National Research Council.

Somen: a very fine, white Japanese wheat noodle.

Star anise: a woody, star-shaped spice, similar in flavor to anise seed and used most often in braised dishes. Ground star anise is a component of Chinese five-spice powder.

Stir fry: to cook small, uniformly cut vegetables, fish or meat over high heat in a little oil, stirring constantly to ensure even cooking in a short time.

Stock: a savory liquid made by simmering aromatic vegetables, herbs and spices — and usually uncooked meat, bones and trimmings — in water. Stock forms a flavor-rich base for sauces.

Straw mushrooms: a cultivated mushroom with pointed caps and a silky texture. Straw mushrooms are usually available in cans or jars; the dried variety must be soaked in very hot water for at least 20 minutes before use. See also Mushrooms, dried Asian.

Sugar snap peas: a variation of garden pea introduced in 1979; when stem and string are removed, the entire pod may be eaten. See also Snow peas.

Sweet chili sauce: any of a group of Asian sauces containing chilies, vinegar, garlic, sugar and salt. The sauce may be used as a condiment to accompany meats, poultry or fish, or it may be included as an ingredient in a dish. Thai varieties, which include seeds and small pieces of chili, are far milder than the ketchup-like sweet chili sauces produced in Malaysia

and Singapore. When sweet chili sauce is unavailable, make it at home by mixing 1 tablespoon each of corn syrup and rice vinegar with 1 to 2 teaspoons of crushed red pepper.

Sweet potato: either of two types of a nutritious tuber grown in the United States. One type has yellowish, mealy flesh; the other has moist, sweet, orange flesh and is often sold as a yam.

Tarragon: a strong herb with a sweet anise taste. Because heat intensifies tarragon's flavor, cooked dishes require smaller amounts.

Thyme: a versatile herb with a zesty, slightly fruity flavor and a strong aroma.

Tomatillo: a small, tart, green, tomato-like fruit vegetable that is frequently used in Mexican dishes. It is covered with a loose, papery husk.

Total fat: an individual's daily intake of polyunsaturated, monounsaturated and saturated fats. Nutritionists recommend that fat constitute no more than 30 percent of a diet. The term as applied in this book refers to the combined fats in a given dish or food.

Transparent noodles: see Beanthread noodles.

Turmeric: a yellow spice from a plant related to ginger, used as a coloring agent and occasionally as a substitute for saffron. Turmeric has a musty odor and a slightly bitter flavor.

Virgin olive oil: see Olive oil.

Wasabi: a Japanese horseradish root, usually sold in powdered form. It is mixed with water to form a fiery green paste, served with noodles or sushi.

Water chestnut: the walnut-size tuber of an aquatic Asian plant, with rough brown skin and white, sweet, crisp flesh. Fresh water chestnuts may be refrigerated for up to two weeks; they must be peeled before use. To store canned water chestnuts, first blanch or rinse them, then refrigerate for as long as three weeks in fresh water changed daily. A crisp, mild vegetable such as jícama or Jerusalem artichoke makes an acceptable substitute.

White pepper: a powder ground from the same dried berry as that used to make black pepper, but with the berry's outer shell removed before grinding, resulting in a milder flavor.

Wonton wrapper: a thin wrapper, about 3 inches square, made of wheat flour and egg; it is used to encase spicy fillings of meat, fish or vegetables.

Yam: see Sweet potato.

Zest: the colored, flavorful outermost layer of citrus-fruit rind, cut or grated free of the bitter white pith that lies beneath it.

Index

Picture Credits

All photographs in this volume were taken by staff photographer Renée Comet unless otherwise indicated below:

2: top and center, Carolyn Wall Rothery. 4: lower left, Michael Latil. 5: upper right, Michael Latil. 9: Rina Ganassa. 12-13: Taran Z. 18: top, Steven Biver; bottom, Taran Z. 20: right, Taran Z. 21, 22: Steven Biver. 23: top, Taran Z; bottom, Steven Biver. 25: Steven Biver. 26: left, Michael Latil; right, Taran Z. 27: Steven Biver. 30: Michael Latil. 32: Steven Biver. 36: Michael Latil. 38: Steven Biver. 39: top, Taran Z; bottom, Steven Biver. 44-45: Taran Z. 51: top, Michael Latil. 60: bottom, Michael Latil. 61: Karan Knauer. 67: Michael Latil. 72: Aldo Tutino. 84: top, Michael Latil. 99: Taran Z. 102-103: Taran Z. 105: Michael Latil. 108: Michael Latil. 111: Michael Latil. 115, 116: Michael Latil. 117: Taran Z. 118-121: Michael Latil. 123: Taran Z. 125, 126: Michael Latil. 127: Taran Z. 129, 130: Michael Latil. 132-136: Michael Latil. 138, 139: Michael Latil.

Props: Cover: measuring cup, Mabel's Kountry Store, Alexandria, Va.; juicer, The Two Harolds Antiques, Alexandria, Va.; napkins, Ken Ceccucci. 6: pot, Portside, Alexandria, Va. 9: spaghetti fork, Bowl & Board, Washington, D.C. 10-11: cruet, 19 Logan Circle; bottles, Wayne Hill; copper pot, strainers, mold and egg basket, Phyllis Van Auken Antiques, Kensington, Md.; copper jug, Susan Johnston; copper ladle, Chenonceau Antiques, Washington, D.C.; stoneware jug, Alayne Berman; slate, Michael Latil. 14: The American Hand Plus, Washington, D.C. 16: serving set, Sharon Farrington. 17: background, Joan Rich, Kensington, Md. 20: Phyllis Van Auken Antiques. 25: King Street Antiques, Alexandria, Va. 28: Liberty, Washington, D.C. 31: Martin's of Georgetown, Washington, D.C. 35: Phyllis Van Auken Antiques. 37: Mary George Kronstadt, Jackie Chalkley, Washington, D.C.; cloth, Sharon Farrington. 41: Edna Giovanelli, Scope Gallery, Torpedo Factory Art Center, Alexandria, Va. 42-43: bowls and red plate, La Cuisinière, Inc., New York, N.Y.; jug and tureen, Susan Johnston; glass jars, Portside; wall tile, la terrine, New York, N.Y.; jar, Caren Pauley; green plate, Silverman Galleries, Alexandria, Va.; tree and planter, Cravens Nursery, Fairfax, Va. 55: lobster trap, U.S. Fish, Kensington, Md. 56: wagon, Cherishables, Washington, D.C. 59: Williams-Sonoma, Washington, D.C. 62: platter, Rob Barnard, Anton Gallery, Washington, D.C.; teapot, Ellen Godwin. 63: pig, Nancy Thomas, Yorktown, Va.; cloth, Chris Swekel. 65: Limor Carrigan, Crofton, Md.; juicer, The Coffee Connection, Washington, D.C. 67: bowl, Sutton Place Gourmet, Washington, D.C.; servers, Bowl & Board. 68-69: pottery, Fran Riecken. 76: Limor Carrigan. 77: background, Wicker World, Washington, D.C. 82: Limor Carrigan. 86: tablecloth, Warehouse Antiques, Alexandria, Va. 88: Maggie Creshkoff, Backlog Pottery, Port Deposit, Md.; colander, Holly Rosenfeld, Torpedo Factory Art Center. 89: Bruce Brett. 93: Nancy Brucks. 97: Joyce Piotrowski; bread, Old Town Bamiyan; background, Ariana Oriental Rugs, Alexandria, Va. 100-101: screen, Trocadero Asian Art, Washington, D.C.; paper, knife and sushi mats, Ginza "Things Japanese," Washington, D.C.; skimmers, Sharon Farrington; marriage basket, China Gallery & Gifts, Washington, D.C.; chopping block, Nittaya Rodsa; furnishings, pottery, boxes, teapot, hat and ladle, Ellen Godwin. 104: Ginza "Things Japanese"; servers, Jerry Newman. 105: Jerry Newman; chopsticks, Full Circle, Alexandria, Va. 106-107: tray, Sharon Farrington. 108: Sharon Farrington. 109: Joan Rich. 111: Ginza "Things Japanese." 113: Sharon Farrington; cloth, Asian Food, Wheaton, Md. 115: bowl, Kirby Rodriquez; tray, Sharon Farrington; plants, Cravens Nursery. 116: plate, Marge Erdman, Hollin Hills Potters, Torpedo Factory Art Center; chopstick rest, Ginza "Things Japanese"; chopsticks, Sharon Farrington. 119: Bowl & Board. 122: plate, Ginns Office Products, Alexandria, Va.; duck and bowl, Sharon Farrington. 124: Valerie Gilman. 125: Ellen Godwin. 126: Sharon Farrington. 128: Ginza "Things Japanese." 132: Ginza "Things Japanese." 133: The Flower Designer, Washington, D.C. 134: La Cuisinière. 139: Martin's of Georgetown.

Acknowledgments

The index for this book was prepared by Barbara Klein. The editors are particularly indebted to Nora Carey, Paris, France; Chong Su Han, Grass Roots Restaurant, Columbia, Md.; Kathy Hardesty, Columbia, Md.; Ken Pierpoint, Owings Mills, Md.; Tajuana Queen, Washington, D.C.; Linda Robertson, Jud Tile, Vienna, Va.; Troiano Marble, Beltsville, Md.; Tina Ujlaki, New York, N.Y.; Phyllis Van Auken Antiques, Kensington, Md.

The editors also thank the following: The American Hand Plus, Washington, D.C.; Stuart Berman, Washington, D.C.; Max Busetti, National Pasta Association, Arlington, Va.; Jackie Chalkley, Washington, D.C.; China Closet, Bethesda, Md.; Nic Colling, Home Produce Company, Alexandria, Va.; Shirley Corriher, Atlanta, Ga.; Sonny Di Martino, Safeway, Alexandria, Va.; Rex Downey, Oxon Hill, Md.; Dennis Drake, Dr. Jacob Exler, Ruth Matthews, U.S. Department of Agriculture, Hyattsville, Md.; Flowers Unique, Inc., Alexandria, Va.; Kitchen Bazaar, Washington, D.C.; Kossow Gourmet Produce, Washington, D.C.; A. Litteri, Inc., Washington, D.C.; Marie Lou, Golden Wok Restaurant, Washington, D.C.; Nick Lyddane, Imperial Produce, Washington, D.C.; Ron Naman, Sutton Place Gourmet, Washington, D.C.; Edward and Robert Nevy, Cumberland Macaroni Manufacturing Company, Cumberland, Md.; Lisa Ownby, Alexandria, Va.; Leon Pinto, Gourmand, Inc., Alexandria, Va.; Joyce Piotrowski, Vienna, Va.; Jerry Purdy, Giant Food, Landover, Md.; Tin T. Quang, East Wind Restaurant, Alexandria, Va.; RT's Restaurant, Alexandria, Va.; James Rzepny, Ticonderoga Farms, Chantilly, Va.; Ronnie Sarragaso, Sutton Place Gourmet, Bethesda, Md.; Straight from the Crate, Inc., Alexandria, Va.; U.S. Fish, Alexandria, Va., and Kensington, Md.; Williams-Sonoma, Washington, D.C. The editors wish to thank the following for their donation of kitchen equipment: Le Creuset, distributed by Schiller & Asmus, Inc., Yemasse, S.C.; Cuisinarts, Inc., Greenwich, Conn.; KitchenAid, Inc., Troy, Ohio; Oster, Milwaukee, Wis.

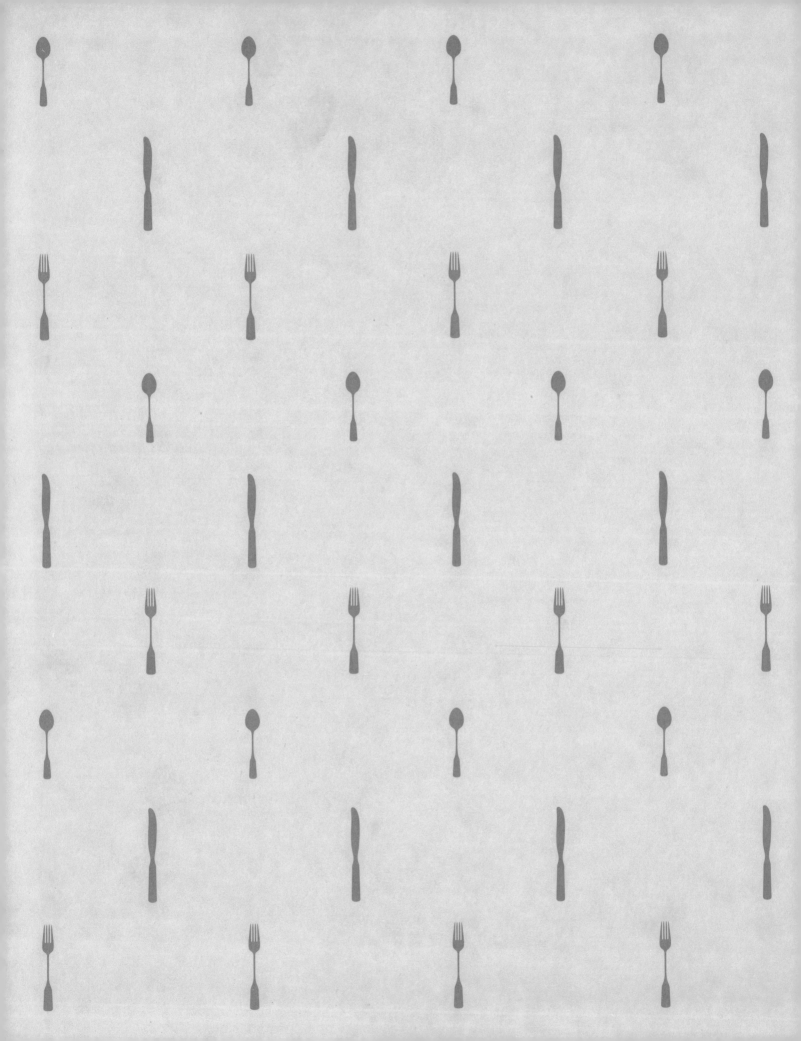